MW01012282

the Jane Goodall Institute

#EATMEATLESS

GOOD FOR ANIMALS, THE EARTH & ALL

the Jane Goodall Institute

#EATMEATLESS

GOOD FOR ANIMALS, THE EARTH & ALL

75+ PLANT-BASED RECIPES TO
NOURISH YOURSELF & HELP THE PLANET

Foreword by Dr. Jane Goodall, DBE,
Founder of the Jane Goodall Institute
and U.N. Messenger of Peace

NewSeed
PRESS

CONTENTS

Mains

Desserts

Basics

FOREWORD
Dr. Jane Goodall, DBE

Every day we live, we have the choice of what kind of impact we want to make. *Choosing to eat differently does not have to be a radical change—small steps will make a difference.* You have the choice to create a better world by considering the positive impact you can make through a plant-based diet. If you're new to the idea, or even if you have been plant-based for a while, this book will inspire you. It demonstrates how easy, accessible, and affordable such a diet can be. More than anything it is intended to help you realize how what we eat really does matter, really does make a difference as more and more people move towards a plant-based diet. When you #EATMEATLESS, it makes a difference for you—for your health, for other people, for the planet, and for the lives of billions of farm animals.

So why does it matter? What difference does it really make? There are three main reasons why you should #EATMEATLESS. Firstly, so that we may eliminate factory farms. I stopped eating meat some 50 years ago when I first learned about factory farms—intensive animal farming. I looked at the piece of meat on my plate and thought, this represents: Fear—Pain—Death. We need to realize that the billions of animals who suffer in factory farms around the globe are individuals with complex emotions, intelligence, and social bonds.

When I first looked into the eyes of a wild chimpanzee, I knew that an intelligent being was looking back at me. I got to know the community members as individuals with different personalities; beings who could use and make tools, form long-term family bonds, and show true altruism. I was reprimanded initially by many scientists who tried to convince me that these attributes were unique to humans—that we were quite different from the rest of the animal kingdom. Eventually, detailed observations and documentary film forced people to abandon that reductionist way of thinking. We are part of and not separated from the rest of the animal kingdom. Cows, pigs, sheep and goats are highly intelligent. Hens, geese, ducks and turkeys can feel fear and pain. What right have we to treat all these animals as though they are mere things put in this world just for us to eat? Pigs, for example, are in fact highly intelligent, comparably to dogs and primates.I have always loved pigs.

It is important to realize that all these domestic farm animals are individuals and their lives have intrinsic value. It's up to us to speak out for them, for they cannot speak for themselves.

In addition, intensive animal farming inflicts terrible damage on the environment and contributes to the climate crisis. The animals must be fed, and large areas of habitat are destroyed for growing grain and for grazing. Studies have shown that it takes more land, water, and energy to produce a pound of animal protein than it does to produce a pound of plant protein. Beef, lamb, and dairy production are the biggest offenders.[1]

Around the globe, fresh water supplies are decreasing and agriculture uses more fresh water than any other human activity.[2] Almost one-third of that water goes towards raising livestock. Cattle ranching is devastating vital rainforests, which, when cut down or burned, release massive amounts of carbon into the atmosphere, contributing to the greenhouse gases responsible for the climate crisis.[3] As livestock digest their food, they release methane, another major greenhouse gas that contributes to climate change. The fossil fuels required to operate farm machinery, produce fertilizer, and transport grain and livestock add to the grim picture. According to a special report by the Intergovernmental Panel on Climate Change, the global livestock sector, which includes growing feed crops, manufacturing fertilizer, and shipping products is responsible for over 14 percent of all greenhouse-gas emissions.[4] Those emissions are driving

[1] Swinburn, Boyd A, Vivica I Kraak, Steven Allender, Vincent J Atkins, Phillip I Baker, Jessica R Bogard, Hannah Brinsden, et al. 2019. "The Global Syndemic of Obesity, Undernutrition, and Climate Change: The Lancet Commission Report." The Lancet 393 (10173): 791–846. https://doi.org/10.1016/s0140-6736(18)32822-8.
[2] Little, Amanda. 2019. *The Fate of Food: What We'll Eat in a Bigger, Hotter, Smarter World* (New York: Harmony Books), 20.
[3] Yale University. 2011. "Cattle Ranching in the Amazon Region | Global Forest Atlas." Yale.Edu. 2011. https://globalforestatlas.yale.edu/amazon/land-use/cattle-ranching
[4] IPCC, [P.R. Shukla, J. Skea, E. Calvo Buendia, V. Masson-Delmotte, H.- O. Pörtner, D. C. Roberts, P. Zhai, R. Slade, S. Connors, R. van Diemen, M. Ferrat, E. Haughey, S. Luz, S. Neogi, M. Pathak, J. Petzold, J. Portugal Pereira, P. Vyas, E. Huntley, K. Kissick, M. Belkacemi, J. Malley, (eds.)]. 2019: *Summary for Policymakers. In: Climate Change and Land: an IPCC special report on climate change, desertification, land degradation, sustainable land management, food security, and greenhouse gas fluxes in terrestrial ecosystems.*

climate change, and in turn, climate change is hastening land degradation and destabilizing the world's food supply.

The estimated time we have left before the damage is irreversible is shrinking, and it is clear we must act, now. Moving to a plant-based diet is one way each one of us can help.

And finally, by choosing to #EATMEATLESS you can help improve your health and the health of many people, especially those employed in the intensive farms or affected by the injustice of the current food system.

Additionally, industrialized animal-agriculture provides some of the worst conditions for employees.[5] Many large companies face existing lawsuits over their factory conditions and practices of poor wages for their marginalized workforce including many people of color and immigrants.[6] Beyond the harm of the industry to employees, cheap animal products are widely available in areas where food deserts reign over fresh produce, continuing to harm the health of those communities.

We must do better.

Despite all of this, I have many reasons for hope—one of which is the remarkable human brain. There have already been so many innovations and ideas to change this system. There are more plant-based food options appearing every single day, and this book is proof that to #EATMEATLESS doesn't mean sacrificing the pleasure, culture, or accessibility of food.

But it all begins with you! *You can help set the standard for a food system that cares about people, animals, and the planet.* So, choose to #EATMEATLESS as this small step can have big results. Imagine the world we could create—one bite at a time.

[5] American Public Health Association. 2017. "Improving Working Conditions for U.S. Farmworkers and Food Production Workers." https://www.apha.org/policies-and-advocacy/public-health-policy-statements/policy-database/2018/01/18/improving-working-conditions.

[6] McConnell, Matt. 2019. "'When We're Dead and Buried, Our Bones Will Keep Hurting' | Workers' Rights Under Threat in US Meat and Poultry Plants." Human Rights Watch. https://www.hrw.org/report/2019/09/04/when-were-dead-and-buried-our-bones-will-keep-hurting/workers-rights-under-threat.

YOUR PLATE & THE PLANET

One of today's most pressing issues is the ongoing destruction of the environment. The forces leading environmental destruction and climate change are generated by an array of activities, often are backed by powerful corporations, and driven by unsustainable global demand.[7] For any one person, the situation can seem overwhelming. If you are feeling frustrated and powerless, there is one simple step you can take to lessen your climate footprint: go plant-based.

"Each decision we make—what we choose to buy, choose to eat, will have an impact on the environment, on animal welfare—and, importantly, on human health." [8]

Changing your consumption of animal products to go plant-based is a small but profound step toward reducing greenhouse-gas emissions and fighting climate change.[9] *No one person can bring climate change to a halt, but many people making small changes can help, and your role as a consumer is important!* [10] So many companies have already shifted greatly to make room for a more eco-conscious plant-based market, driven by people like you! You don't have to be wealthy, and you don't have to devote your entire life to activism. Simply eating more plant-based is a potent force for change that you can practice every day. And eating plant-based

[7] Ekwurzel, B., Boneham, J., Dalton, M.W. et al. 2017. *The rise in global atmospheric CO2, surface temperature, and sea level from emissions traced to major carbon producers.* Climatic Change 144, 579–590.

[8] Goodall, McAvoy, and Hudson, *Harvest for Hope*, xxiii–xxiv.

[9] IPCC, [P.R. Shukla, et al]. *Summary for Policymakers.*

[10] McMullen, S., Halteman, M.C. 2019. *Against Inefficacy Objections: the Real Economic Impact of Individual Consumer Choices on Animal Agriculture.* Food ethics 2, 93–110.

is as much about reducing animal products as it is about learning about how food systems and your consumer decisions affect the planet. *Try buying local (depending on the type of typical transportation for average foods by distance) and organic when available, affordable, and in season (or growing your own!).* These are all good ways to focus on sustainability and your carbon footprint, but above all what you eat matters most—going plant-based really does have a big impact![11]

[11] IPCC, [P.R. Shukla, et al]. *Summary for Policymakers.*

YOUR FOOD &
THE FACTORIES

Our current system of industrial farming, with its heavy reliance on fossil fuels, chemicals, water, and land, is not sustainable. This system is poisoning our air and water, contributing to poor health, deepening social inequity, and concentrating control of our food in the hands of a few.[12] Industrial farming is responsible for a significant percentage of global greenhouse-gas emissions.[13] To produce cheap and abundant food, large factory farms rely on chemicals and intensive, concentrated methods for raising animals.[14]

"There has never been a time when it is more crucial for us to carefully consider where our food is coming from and how it is grown, raised, and harvested—so that we can make informed efforts to purchase the right things. For our choices will not only affect our own health but also the environment and animal welfare." [15]

Even with all the "efficiency" built into industrial farms, the animal-product-based model is not efficient—in particular, our unsustainable use of land and deforestation is profoundly contributing to climate change. Vast swaths of land are cleared and sprayed with fertilizers and pesticides to grow the plants that are then harvested and transported to be used as animal feed. Animals are fed and watered and produce waste before being transported to slaughter. All of this requires

---

[12] Woodall, Patrick, and Tyler L. Shannon. 2018. "Monopoly Power Corrodes Choice and Resiliency in the Food System." The Antitrust Bulletin 63 (2): 198–221. https://journals.sagepub.com/doi/10.1177/0003603X18770063.

[13] Hersher, Rebecca, and Allison Aubrey. 2019. "To Slow Global Warming, U.N. Warns Agriculture Must Change." NPR.Org. August 8, 2019. https://www.npr.org/sections/thesalt/2019/08/08/748416223/to-slow-global-warming-u-n-warns-agriculture-must-change.

[14] Allen, A. M., & Hof, A. R. 2019. *Paying the price for the meat we eat*. Environmental Science & Policy, 97, 90-94.

[15] Goodall, McAvoy, and Hudson, *Harvest for Hope*, 280.

massive amounts of water and fossil fuels to plant, harvest, transport, process, and refrigerate the final product. Meat and dairy production have the largest impact on the environment.[16] Plant-based foods have an impact on the environment as well, but in general, it takes less land, energy, and water to produce a pound of plant protein than it does to produce a pound of animal protein.[17]

"One way in which we can truly make a difference is to think about what we eat. Each decision we make—what we choose to buy, choose to eat, will have an impact on the environment, on animal welfare—and, importantly, on human health."

Fundamentally, factory farms are horrifically cruel and demonstrate the worst of our humanity in the mistreatment of other animals. In 1960, Dr. Goodall transformed our understanding of our closest living relatives—wild chimpanzees. Her findings shined a light on their tremendous intelligence, emotions, and ability for compassion. Since that time, an extraordinary amount of research has reflected an entirely new way of understanding non-human animals—one of nuance and sentience. Conditions in factory farms not only remove the rights of animals to a life of dignity but also subject them to the most heinous, violent conditions.[18] Helping shift this industry away from cruelty can start by pledging to #EATMEATLESS. The more you choose plants, the more you fill the world with hope for animals!

[16] Swinburn, Boyd A, et al. "The Global Syndemic of Obesity".

[17] Shepon, Alon, Gidon Eshel, Elad Noor, and Ron Milo. 2018. "The Opportunity Cost of Animal Based Diets Exceeds All Food Losses." Proceedings of the National Academy of Sciences 115 (15): 3804–9. https://doi.org/10.1073/pnas.1713820115.

[18] Fiber-Ostrow, Pamela, and Jarret S. Lovell. 2016. "Behind a Veil of Secrecy: Animal Abuse, Factory Farms, and Ag-Gag Legislation." Contemporary Justice Review 19 (2): 230–49. https://www.tandfonline.com/doi/full/10.1080/10282580.2016.1168257.

SMALL SOLUTIONS CAN
SAVE OUR FOOD SYSTEM

Making your diet more plant-based and planet-friendly doesn't have to mean increased cost or hassle. Replace your breakfast of bacon and eggs with a vegetable frittata. Switch up dinner meals by grilling vegetables instead of steak for an entrée, or prepare a hearty salad instead of meatballs. Once you start to #EATMEATLESS, it will become second nature.

"Every time an individual makes such a change in his or her lifestyle, the number of people eating ethically and healthily increases—by one." [19]

Choosing a plant-based lifestyle is as much about choosing foods that are good for you and animals as it is about making consumer decisions that are good for the planet overall. If you have one nearby, check out your local farmers' markets and other sources for locally grown food. When you find a market you like, get to know your farmers. They are a valuable part of the community and can guide you to what's fresh and good. You can also learn how to grow your own food, even if you don't have large or any outdoor space. Saving the bottoms of many vegetables like lettuce and placing them in water will help regrow food easily. And if you don't have access to farmers' markets or fresh produce, stock your pantry with beans, nuts, seeds, and other plant-based staples—so many nutritious and delicious plant-based foods are surprisingly very low cost. There are also many new options for community supported agriculture groups (CSA) and fresh, local food delivery. When you take this approach, you'll find yourself getting more in touch with the seasons and developing a feel for what will be harvested at different times of the year. Every season brings

---

[19] Goodall, McAvoy, and Hudson, *Harvest for Hope*, 284.

an abundance of colorful, hearty fruits and vegetables. A diet grounded in fruits, vegetables, whole grains, tubers, and legumes—accompanied by noodles, nuts, herbs, and other foods—gives you countless options for a delicious, nourishing, and healthful way of eating that's good for you, other animals, and the planet.

"Every individual has a role to play. Every individual makes a difference."

The recipe collection that follows includes tasty and nutritious dishes for every meal of the day. For breakfast, you'll find buckwheat muffins with blueberries (easy to make in advance), tofu scramble wraps with spinach and sunflower seeds, and a quinoa and nondairy yogurt bowl with marmalade drizzle and pistachios. Soups and salads include creamy carrot soup with carrot top gremolata (using the carrot from tip to top), cremini mushroom and barley soup with thyme, new potato and radish salad with mustard-dill vinaigrette, and winter gado gado salad with peanut sauce. Main-course options are inspired by cuisines from around the world: Indonesian-style salad with tempeh, black bean–avocado sopes, pan-fried falafel with cumin and garlic, roasted vegetable strudel, and rice with chipotle and kidney beans. Round out your meals with desserts ranging from mocha brownies and apple-cranberry crumble bars to candied orange peel dipped in chocolate and aquafaba chocolate mousse.

You can be a climate-change activist in your own kitchen. When you #EATMEATLESS, you not only nuture your health and well-being, you also help care for the planet.

"Yes, collectively we, the people, are the force that can lead to change." [20]

---

[20] Goodall, McAvoy, and Hudson, *Harvest for Hope*, 284.

BREAKFAST

"What the exciting boom in organic foods has taught us is that we, the people, by virtue of the products we purchase—and those that we don't—can change global agricultural practices." —Jane

TOFU SCRAMBLE WRAPS WITH SPINACH & SPICED SUNFLOWER SEEDS

Leave the eggs to the hens and try a tofu scramble for breakfast. In this recipe, the addition of chickpea flour and turmeric gives the scramble an eggy texture and color. Sustainably grown tofu has a low carbon footprint and its protein level is high, so buy a block or two next time you go shopping. If you want to eat the scramble straight out of the pan with toast, that works, too.

FOR THE SPICED SUNFLOWER SEEDS

Raw sunflower seeds, ½ cup (2 oz/60 g)

Avocado oil, ¼ teaspoon

Smoked paprika, ¼ teaspoon

Sea salt

Extra-firm tofu, 12 oz (340 g)

Chickpea flour, ¼ cup (¾ oz/20 g)

Dried basil, 2 teaspoons

Ground turmeric, ½ teaspoon

Freshly ground pepper

Tamari, 1 tablespoon

Apple cider vinegar, 2 teaspoons

Vegan mustard, 1 teaspoon

Green onions, 3, thinly sliced

Carrot, 1 large, grated

Avocado oil, 2 teaspoons

Whole-wheat tortillas (9 inches/23 cm), 4

Baby spinach, 2 cups (2 oz/60 g) loosely packed

1. To make the spiced sunflower seeds, have ready a small bowl. In a small skillet, heat the sunflower seeds over medium-high heat, shaking and stirring until they are fragrant and lightly toasted, 3–5 minutes. Sprinkle with the oil, paprika, and ¼ teaspoon salt and stir quickly to coat. Transfer to the bowl to cool slightly before using in the wraps.

2. To press the tofu, drain, wrap in a thick kitchen towel, and place on a plate. Place a heavy pan or cutting board on top and let stand for about 5 minutes. Unwrap and pat dry with another towel. Coarsely crumble into a large bowl.

3. Sprinkle the chickpea flour, basil, turmeric, and ½ teaspoon pepper over the tofu. Add the tamari, vinegar, and mustard. Turn gently with your hands to mix, crushing the tofu to the size of scrambled-egg curds. Fold in the green onions and carrot.

4. Preheat a large sauté pan or skillet over medium-high heat. When the pan is hot, add the oil and distribute evenly. Add the tofu mixture and use a metal offset spatula to turn the mixture as it cooks. Scrape the bottom of the pan as you turn the scramble and cook until the tofu is lightly browned, about 5 minutes.

5. For each wrap, place a tortilla on a plate and put one-fourth of the spinach in the middle. Top with one-fourth of the hot scramble. Sprinkle with 2 tablespoons of the spiced sunflower seeds, then fold in the sides of the tortilla and roll up. Repeat with the rest of the tortillas. Serve right away.

MAKES 4 SERVINGS

BANANA PANCAKES WITH SEASONAL FRUIT SYRUP

White whole-wheat flour is made from a variety of wheat that has a pale outer bran layer, so it looks like white flour but has all the benefits of whole-grain wheat. If you can't find it, substitute whole-wheat pastry flour. You can use a ripe banana for these pancakes, and it will caramelize nicely in the hot pan, a perfect foil for the fruity syrup.

Fresh or thawed frozen berries or fruit, 2 cups (8 oz/225 g), plus fresh berries for garnish

Maple syrup, ¼ cup (2¾ oz/80 g)

White whole-wheat flour or whole-wheat pastry flour, 1½ cups (6½ oz/185 g)

Brown sugar, 1 tablespoon

Baking powder, 1 teaspoon

Baking soda, ½ teaspoon

Sea salt

Unsweetened nondairy milk, 1½ cups (12 fl oz/350 ml) plus 1 tablespoon

Canola oil, 2 tablespoons

Apple cider vinegar, 1 tablespoon

Ground flax seeds, 2 tablespoons

Ripe banana, 1 large, peeled and thinly sliced

MAKES 4 SERVINGS

1. To make the fruit syrup, in a 1-quart (950-ml) pot, combine the fruit and maple syrup and set over medium heat. Bring to a boil and cook, stirring often, until the fruit is soft and the syrup is slightly thickened, 2–5 minutes. Keep warm over very low heat while you make the pancakes.

2. If desired, preheat the oven to 200°F (95°C). Place a heat-safe platter or pan in the oven to keep the cooked pancakes warm.

3. In a large bowl, whisk together the flour, brown sugar, baking powder, baking soda, and ½ teaspoon salt. In a medium bowl, whisk together the nondairy milk, oil, vinegar, and ground flax and let stand for 5 minutes for the flax to gel. Stir the nondairy milk mixture into the flour mixture just until all the flour is moistened.

4. Warm a griddle or a large nonstick frying pan over high heat. Spray with vegetable oil spray just before adding the batter. Stir the batter again, then use a ¼-cup (60-ml) measure to scoop the batter onto the hot griddle, leaving 1 inch (2.5 cm) of space between the cakes. Place 3 slices of banana on top of each cake and tap down with a spatula to adhere. When the batter starts to bubble, reduce the heat to medium. When the edges of a pancake look dry and cooked and the surface is covered with holes, about 2 minutes, flip the cake. Cook for 2 minutes on the second side. Transfer the finished pancakes to the platter in the oven, if using, while you finish cooking the rest of the pancakes, using more vegetable oil spray as needed.

5. Place 3–4 pancakes on each plate, top with one-fourth of the fruit syrup, and garnish with berries. Serve right away.

QUINOA BOWLS WITH MARMALADE DRIZZLE & PISTACHIOS

Some quinoa is grown in North America now, in addition to its native Peru. That decreases the miles it must travel to reach your table. These bowls make good use of the versatile grainlike seed, a great source of protein, fiber, B vitamins, and minerals for plant-based diners. Use an apple, pear, or whatever fruit is local and in season to make the freshest, lowest-impact bowl.

Quinoa, ½ cup (4 oz/115 g), rinsed and drained

Orange marmalade, ¼ cup (2½ oz/70 g)

Orange juice, 2 tablespoons

Apple or pear, 1 large, halved, cored, and sliced

Plain oat milk yogurt or other nondairy yogurt, 1 cup (8 oz/225 g)

Roasted pistachios, 2 tablespoons, chopped

MAKES 2 SERVINGS

1. In a small pot, bring ¾ cup water (6 fl oz/180 ml) to a boil over high heat. Add the quinoa. Return to a boil and then reduce the heat to low, cover, and cook until the liquid is absorbed, about 15 minutes. Uncover, fluff, and let cool. (The quinoa can be made a day ahead and refrigerated, tightly covered.)

2. To make the bowls, place the marmalade in a small bowl and stir in the orange juice. Spread the quinoa across 2 shallow bowls and arrange half a sliced apple over each. Place half of the nondairy yogurt in the center of each bowl and drizzle the marmalade mixture over the top. Sprinkle each bowl with 1 tablespoon pistachios and serve.

VEGGIE-CHICKPEA FRITTATA MUFFIN CUPS

Here's a breakfast that can be made ahead and reheated, or packed to take along. Derived from sustainable, inexpensive beans, chickpea flour is a whole-food, high-fiber, high-protein stand-in for chicken eggs. Black salt, or kala nemak, is a sulfurous salt from India that makes plant-based dishes like this taste eggy. If you can't find it, just use Himalayan pink salt or another salt.

Olive oil, 1 tablespoon

Yellow onion, 1 cup (4 oz/115 g) chopped

Cauliflower, 1 cup (4 oz/115 g), chopped

Baby spinach, 2 cups (2 oz/60 g) loosely packed

Tomato, 1, chopped

Sea salt

Chickpea flour, 1½ cups (4½ oz/130 g)

Black salt, 1 teaspoon

Freshly ground pepper

MAKES 9 MINI FRITTATAS

1. Preheat the oven to 375°F (190°C). Grease 9 standard muffin cups with 1 teaspoon of the oil.

2. In a large sauté pan, warm the remaining 2 teaspoons olive oil over medium-high heat. Add the onion and cauliflower and cook, stirring occasionally and reducing the heat to medium when the vegetables start to sizzle. When the cauliflower is tender, about 4 minutes, remove the pan from the heat. Stir in the spinach, tomato, and ½ teaspoon sea salt and let stand until the spinach wilts.

3. In a medium bowl, whisk together the chickpea flour, black salt, ½ teaspoon pepper, and 1½ cups (12 fl oz/350 ml) water. Stir the cooked vegetables into the chickpea mixture, then scoop scant ½-cup (115-g) portions into the prepared muffin cups. Smooth the tops.

4. Bake until the tops are cracked and feel firm when pressed, about 45 minutes. Cool in the pan on a rack for 5 minutes. Serve warm or at room temperature. The muffin cups can be stored, tightly covered, in the refrigerator, for up to 4 days.

SWEET POTATOES WITH NONDAIRY YOGURT & MAPLE PUMPKIN SEEDS

This departure from breakfast grains like oatmeal makes a meal around sustainable sweet potatoes. These inexpensive spuds are rich in beta-carotene, vitamins, minerals, and fiber, and they boast a natural sweetness that is perfect in a bowl with nondairy yogurt and toppings. Many nondairy yogurts are now available, made with oat, coconut, and other unsweetened nondairy milks.

Sweet potatoes, 1 lb (450 g), cut into ½-inch (12-mm) cubes

Raw pumpkin seeds (pepitas), ½ cup (2 oz/60 g)

Maple syrup, 1 tablespoon, plus more for serving (optional)

Sea salt

Plain oat milk yogurt or other nondairy yogurt, 4 cups (32 oz/1 kg)

MAKES 4 SERVINGS

1. In a pot large enough to hold a steamer basket, bring water to a boil. Place the sweet potatoes in the steamer and cook until very tender when pierced with a paring knife, about 10 minutes. Remove from the steamer and let cool slightly.

2. Have ready a small plate. In a small sauté pan, heat the pumpkin seeds over medium-high heat. Swirl the pan and toss the seeds until they start to pop and smell toasty, about 3 minutes. Remove from the heat and drizzle with the maple syrup. Add a pinch of salt, quickly stir to coat, then transfer to the plate to cool.

3. Divide the sweet potato cubes and nondairy yogurt evenly among bowls. Sprinkle each bowl with 2 tablespoons maple pumpkin seeds. Drizzle with more maple syrup, if desired, and serve.

BLUEBERRY BUCKWHEAT MUFFINS

If you have only encountered buckwheat in pancakes, these muffins will be a revelation. Buckwheat gives the muffins a purplish tint that complements the blue of the berries, and all that color is a sure sign of antioxidants. The nutty-tasting sustainable grain grows in poor soils and delivers higher mineral levels than wheat or rice.

Whole-wheat pastry flour, 1½ cups
(6½ oz/185 g)

Buckwheat flour, ¾ cup
(3 oz/90 g)

Organic sugar, 1 cup (7 oz/200 g)

Baking powder, 1 teaspoon

Baking soda, ½ teaspoon

Sea salt

Lemon zest, finely grated,
1 tablespoon

Unsweetened nondairy milk, ¾ cup
(6 fl oz/180 ml)

Lemon juice, 2 tablespoons

Ground flax seeds, 2 tablespoons

Avocado oil, ½ cup (4 fl oz/120 ml)

Blueberries, 1½ cups (6 oz/170 g)

Turbinado sugar, 3 tablespoons

MAKES 12 MUFFINS

1. Preheat the oven to 350°F (180°C). Line 12 standard muffin cups with paper liners. Grease the top of the pan so the muffin tops won't stick.

2. In a large bowl, whisk together the whole-wheat and buckwheat flours, organic sugar, baking powder, baking soda, ½ teaspoon salt, and lemon zest.

3. In a medium bowl, stir together the nondairy milk, lemon juice, and ground flax. Let stand for 5 minutes for the flax to gel. Stir in the oil. Add the nondairy milk mixture to the flour mixture and stir until almost combined. Add the blueberries and fold in gently.

4. Use a ⅓-cup (80-ml) measure to scoop the batter into the prepared muffin cups, dividing any leftover batter among them. Smooth the tops and sprinkle evenly with the turbinado sugar.

5. Bake until a toothpick inserted into the center of a muffin comes out clean, about 30 minutes. Cool in the pan on a rack for 10 minutes, then transfer the muffins to the rack to cool completely.

SPELT & CHIA SEED BISCUITS

Spelt, a variety of wheat, is a rich source of protein and dietary fiber. It has a sweet, nutty flavor and makes a tasty, tender biscuit. Here, chilled coconut oil stands in for butter, delivering a buttery flakiness and mouthfeel that is purely plant-based.

Spelt flour or whole-wheat pastry flour, 2 cups (9 oz/250 g), plus more for dusting

Organic sugar, 2 tablespoons

Baking soda, 1 teaspoon

Baking powder, 1 teaspoon

Sea salt

Coconut oil, 6 tablespoons (3 fl oz/90 ml), melted, measured, and chilled

Unsweetened nondairy milk, ¾ cup (6 fl oz/180 ml)

Apple cider vinegar, 1 teaspoon

Chia seeds, ¼ cup (1¾ oz/50 g)

MAKES 12 BISCUITS

1. Preheat the oven to 400°F (200°C). Line a rimmed baking sheet with parchment paper.

2. In a large bowl, whisk together the flour, sugar, baking soda, baking powder, and 1 teaspoon salt. Using a grater, shred the cold coconut oil into the flour mixture. Toss to coat the shreds with the flour mixture and use your fingers to work it in a bit.

3. In a small bowl, whisk together the nondairy milk, vinegar, and chia seeds. Let stand for 5 minutes for the chia seeds to gel, then quickly stir into the flour mixture. When the mixture is just coming together, scrape it out onto a well-floured work surface. Using floured hands, flatten the dough into a rectangle about 8 inches (20 cm) long, 4 inches (10 cm) wide, and ¾ inch (2 cm) thick. Using a bench knife or chef's knife, make 2 evenly spaced cuts across the width and 3 across the length of the rectangle to create 12 rectangular biscuits.

4. Place the biscuits at least 1 inch (2.5 cm) apart on the prepared baking sheet. Bake until golden brown, about 15 minutes. Serve warm.

Recipe note

Despite their small size, chia seeds pack a nutritional punch. With a wealth of micronutrients—including calcium, magnesium, and phosphate—plus antioxidants, fiber, and protein, chia seeds are mostly tasteless and can be thrown into many dishes, from salads to desserts.

PUMPKIN BAKED OATS WITH FLAX SEEDS

Oatmeal is a classic for breakfast, packed with nutrients for pennies per bowl. In this easy preparation, you'll add a healthy vegetable in the form of pumpkin, and flax seed thickens the mixture while delivering omega-3 fats. Slice and reheat leftovers, and serve with a scoop of plant-based yogurt.

Pumpkin or winter squash purée, 1 cup (8 oz/225 g)

Maple syrup, ½ cup (5½ oz/155 g)

Ground cinnamon, 1½ teaspoons

Ground allspice, ½ teaspoon

Ground cloves, ½ teaspoon

Ground nutmeg, ¼ teaspoon

Rolled oats, 1½ cups (4½ oz/130 g)

Unsweetened nondairy milk, 2 cups (16 fl oz/475 ml)

Warm water, 1 cup (8 fl oz/240 ml)

Ground flax seeds, ¼ cup (¾ oz/24 g)

Vanilla extract, 1 teaspoon

Sea salt

Raisins, cranberries, or other dried fruit, ½ cup (3 oz/90 g)

MAKES 5 SERVINGS

1. Preheat the oven to 400°F (200°C). Have ready a 2-quart (1.9-l) baking dish with a cover.

2. In a medium bowl, whisk together the pumpkin, maple syrup, cinnamon, allspice, cloves, and nutmeg. Set aside.

3. In a large sauté pan, heat the oats over medium-high heat. Swirl the oats in the pan until they smell toasty, about 3 minutes. Transfer to the baking dish and cover.

4. In the same pan, heat the pumpkin mixture, stirring frequently, until hot and bubbling, about 5 minutes. Whisk in the nondairy milk, warm water, ground flax, vanilla, and ½ teaspoon salt and bring to a boil. Pour over the oats in the baking dish and stir to mix. Sprinkle the raisins over the top.

5. Cover and bake until the oats are thick and bubbling around the edges, about 30 minutes. Stir well and let stand for 5 minutes before serving in bowls. The oats can be stored, tightly covered in the refrigerator, for up to 4 days.

ON JANE'S JOURNEY TO PLANT-BASED

For Jane, the choice to go plant-based came about for a myriad of reasons, both personal and evidence-based. Born and raised in Bournemouth, England, Jane has shared that she was born loving animals and has cherished childhood memories of a holiday spent on a farm outside of London. When she was a toddler, she even brought worms to bed, something her mother had to explain to her would cause them to die, to her great dismay. From this point on, and throughout her young adulthood, Jane was preoccupied with being around animals to understand and write books about them. She even snuck into a henhouse when she was a little girl to watch how a hen laid an egg for hours, disappearing long enough to cause her mother call the police and report her missing. In the 1960s and 1970s, Jane's groundbreaking studies on wild chimpanzees forever altered the way we see other animals. In the 1970s, she first learned about the horrors of factory farming in Peter Singer's seminal book *Animal Liberation*.

"I can still remember how I felt when I closed Singer's book. There was a sort of numbness in my mind. I knew I would not be able to keep from thinking about the images conjured by the pages I had just read. When I saw meat on my plate, from that moment on, I should think of pain-fear-death. How horrible.

And so it was clear. I would eat no more meat."[1]

[1] Goodall, McAvoy, and Hudson, *Harvest for Hope*, 138–139.
[2] IPCC, [P.R. Shukla, et al]. *Summary for Policymakers*.

Besides her love for animals and her disgust with factory farming practices, Jane's decision was based on its impact on people and the planet. And in addition, there are the resources and labor used to transport, slaughter, process, and distribute the animal to a consumer's plate. *Meat is simply not a humane or efficient way to feed the planet.*[2]

SOUPS

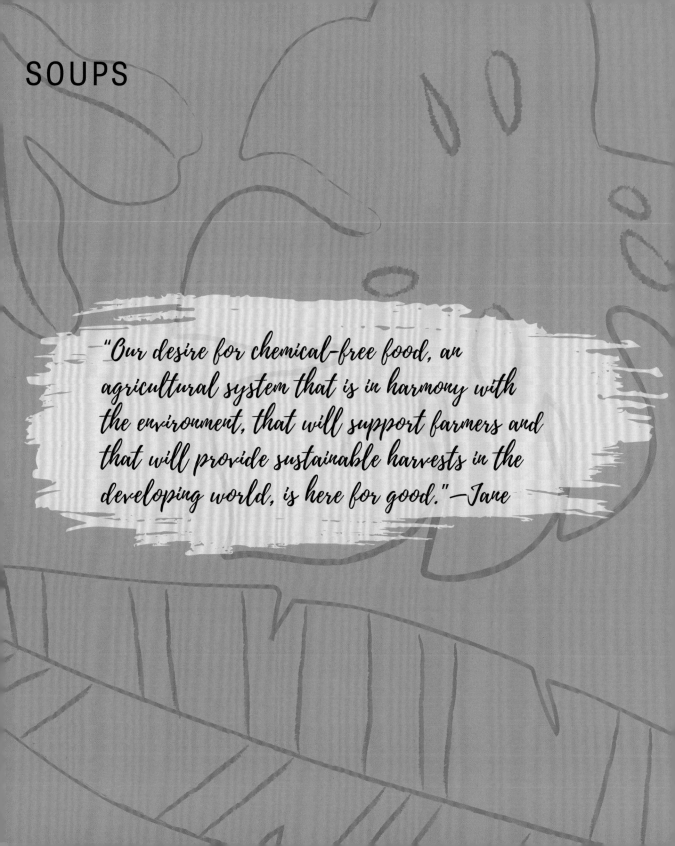

"Our desire for chemical-free food, an agricultural system that is in harmony with the environment, that will support farmers and that will provide sustainable harvests in the developing world, is here for good." —Jane

CHILLED SPICY CUCUMBER GAZPACHO

When the farmers' market is in full summer glory, bring home a few juicy cucumbers to make this refreshing chilled soup. The light and breezy vegetables are blended with healthful extra-virgin olive oil to create a texture that is almost dairylike. Cucumbers are a delicious way to stay hydrated and also contain the crucial mineral potassium, which may help reduce blood pressure.

English cucumbers, 1½ lb (680 g), peeled, seeded, and coarsely chopped

Extra-virgin olive oil, ¾ cup (6 fl oz/180 ml) plus 1 tablespoon, plus more for drizzling

Ice water, ½ cup (4 fl oz/120 ml)

Garlic, 1 small clove

Apple cider vinegar, ¼ cup (2 fl oz/60 ml) plus 2 teaspoons

Lemon juice, 1 tablespoon

Sea salt

Shallot, 1 small, finely diced

Jalapeño chile, 1 small, seeded and finely chopped

Fresh basil, 1 tablespoon finely chopped

MAKES 4 SERVINGS

1. In a blender, combine 4 cups (1¼ lb/570 g) of the cucumbers, the ¾ cup (6 fl oz/180 ml) of the oil, the ice water, garlic, the ¼ cup (2 fl oz/60 ml) vinegar, and the lemon juice and blend until smooth. Pour into a serving bowl and season to taste with salt. Cover and refrigerate for at least 1 hour or up to overnight.

2. In a small bowl, stir together the shallot, the remaining 2 teaspoons vinegar, and a pinch of salt. Let stand for 10 minutes. Stir in the remaining ½ cup (8 oz/230 g) cucumbers, the jalapeño, basil, and the remaining 1 tablespoon oil. Season with salt.

3. Ladle the soup into chilled bowls. Garnish with the jalapeño mixture and drizzle with oil. Serve right away.

SUMMER VEGETABLE MINESTRONE

Peak-of-summer locally grown produce is the freshest and most nutritious, and practically seasons itself. All the cook needs to do is show off the vegetables' vibrant flavors with an easy soup like this one. If you are making the soup ahead of time, don't add the pasta, as it will soak up the broth and become mushy. Instead, wait and cook the pasta just before serving. Distribute it evenly into the bowls, and pour the reheated soup over the top.

Extra-virgin olive oil, 2 tablespoons

Yellow onion, 1 large, chopped

Carrots, 2 large, sliced

Garlic, 2 cloves, chopped

Dried basil, 1 teaspoon

Dried oregano, 1 teaspoon

Fennel seeds, ½ teaspoon

Vegetable broth, 4 cups
(32 fl oz/950 ml)

Tomatoes, 4 large, chopped, with their juices

Chickpeas, 1 can (15 oz/425 g), drained and rinsed

Kidney beans, 1 can (15 oz/425 g), drained and rinsed

Zucchini, 1, quartered lengthwise and sliced

Sea salt and freshly ground pepper

Kale, 1 bunch, ribs removed and thinly sliced, and leaves chopped

Fresh flat-leaf parsley, ½ cup
(¾ oz/20 g) chopped

Orzo, ½ cup (3½ oz/100 g)
(optional)

MAKES 6 SERVINGS

1. In a large pot, warm the oil over medium-high heat. Add the onion and carrots and cook, stirring occasionally, until starting to soften, about 5 minutes. Add the garlic, basil, oregano, fennel seeds, broth, tomatoes and their juices, chickpeas, kidney beans, zucchini, and ½ teaspoon each salt and pepper. Cover and bring to a boil, then reduce the heat to low and cook until the vegetables are tender, about 10 minutes. Remove from the heat. Stir in the kale and parsley and let stand, covered, until the kale is wilted, about 2 minutes.

2. Meanwhile, if using the orzo, bring a saucepan of salted water to a boil. Add the orzo and cook until al dente according to package instructions. Drain well. Stir the orzo into the finished soup.

3. Ladle the soup into bowls and serve right away.

CREAMY ASPARAGUS SOUP WITH CRUNCHY ALMOND GARNISH

When asparagus is in season, feast on it in this creamy soup. Asparagus is a perennial crop, which means there is less energy wasted—just a harvest when the spears emerge. Used as a thickener here, millet is a whole grain that grows well in dry conditions and is pest and disease resistant.

Asparagus, 1 lb (450 g)

Extra-virgin olive oil, 1 teaspoon

Yellow onion, 1 cup (4 oz/115 g) chopped

Millet, ¼ cup (2 oz/30 g)

Vegetable broth, 1½ cups (12 fl oz/350 ml)

Arugula, 2 cups (2 oz/60 g) loosely packed

Sea salt and freshly ground pepper

Unsweetened nondairy milk, 1½ cups (12 fl oz/350 ml)

Fresh flat-leaf parsley, ½ cup (¾ oz/20 g) chopped

Slivered almonds, ¼ cup (¾ oz/20 g), toasted

MAKES 4 SERVINGS

1. Trim the tough ends from the asparagus. Cut off the tips and reserve. Chop the remaining spears. In a large pot, warm the oil over medium heat. Add the onion and cook, stirring occasionally, until tender, about 5 minutes. Add the chopped asparagus (not the tips), millet, and broth. Bring to a boil over high heat, then reduce the heat to low, cover, and simmer, until the millet is very soft, about 25 minutes.

2. Meanwhile, set up a steamer and steam the asparagus tips for about 2 minutes, until just tender. Set aside.

3. Transfer the millet-asparagus mixture to a blender. Add the arugula and blend until combined. Scrape down the sides of the blender and add ½ teaspoon each salt and pepper. With the machine running, pour the nondairy milk through the lid and blend until smooth and well mixed. Transfer the soup back to the pot and warm gently, if needed.

4. Ladle the soup into bowls and garnish each serving with asparagus tips, parsley, and 1 tablespoon almonds. Serve right away.

CORN SOUP WITH BASIL

Corn on the cob is one of the joys of summer, boiled or grilled and slathered with nondairy butter. It's also lovely in this velvety soup, where you'll tease out the hidden flavor and nutrients from the corncobs and vegetable trims by first making a simple stock. Once the stock vegetables have released their essence, they can go into the compost bin.

FOR THE STOCK

Corn on the cob, 2 ears

Carrots, 2 large

Zucchini, 1

Yellow onions, 2 large

Fresh flat-leaf parsley, 1 bunch

Cherry tomatoes, 1 cup
(6 oz/170 g) halved

Garlic, 2 cloves, halved

Black peppercorns, ½ teaspoon

Sea salt

Bay leaves, 2

FOR THE SOUP

Avocado oil, 1 tablespoon

Cooked chickpeas, 1½ cups
(10½ oz/300 g), with ¾ cup
(6 fl oz/180 ml) cooking liquid

Roma tomato, 1 large, chopped

Fresh basil, ½ cup (¾ oz/20 g)
chopped

Sea salt and freshly ground pepper

MAKES 6 SERVINGS

1. To make the stock, fill a large pot with 6 cups (48 fl oz/1.4 l) water and place over medium heat. As you prep the vegetables, add the trims to the water. Shuck the corn and put the husks in the pot. Cut the kernels from the cobs and reserve; add the cobs to the pot. Peel, trim, and chop the carrots, adding the peels and trims to the pot and reserving the chopped carrots. Trim and slice the zucchini, adding the trims to the pot and reserving the sliced zucchini. Leaving the skin on, cut 1 onion into thick slices and add to the pot. Trim and chop the remaining onion, adding the trims to the pot and reserving the chopped onion. Cut the parsley leaves away from the stems and add the stems to the pot, reserving the leaves. Add the cherry tomatoes, garlic, peppercorns, ½ teaspoon salt, and bay leaves to the pot.

2. Bring the contents of the pot to a boil over high heat, then reduce the heat to maintain a gentle simmer. Cover and cook for 45 minutes, over low heat so the stock doesn't boil, which would make it turn bitter. Strain the stock, reserving the liquid.

3. While the stock simmers, start the soup. In a medium pot, warm the oil over medium-high heat. Add the reserved chopped onion and carrots and sauté, reducing the heat when the vegetables start to sizzle. Stir occasionally, over low heat, until the onion is golden and the carrots are soft, about 10 minutes.

4. When the stock is done, place the empty pot back on the stove. Add the sautéed onion and carrots, the reserved zucchini, the chickpeas and their cooking liquid, and the Roma tomato. Bring to a boil over medium-high heat, then reduce to a simmer. Cook until the vegetables are tender, about 10 minutes.

5. Chop the reserved parsley leaves and add them and the basil to the pot. Season the soup to taste with salt and pepper. Ladle into bowls and serve right away.

CREAMY CARROT SOUP
WITH CARROT-TOP GREMOLATA

Don't just compost those carrot tops! They have a peppery, parsley-like flavor and are perfect for making a zingy seasoning mixture. Sweet, earthy carrots are one of the most healthful vegetables, and they are also an eminently sustainable crop. This soup is thickened with millet, a gluten-free whole grain that adds fiber and minerals.

Carrots, 1 lb (450 g), peeled and sliced

Yellow onion, 1 small, coarsely chopped

Garlic, 3 large cloves

Millet or white rice, 3 tablespoons

Unsweetened nondairy milk, 1 cup (8 fl oz/240 ml)

Dried thyme, 1 teaspoon

Sea salt and freshly ground pepper

FOR THE GREMOLATA

Carrot tops or fresh flat-leaf parsley leaves, 1 cup (1 oz/30 g), loosely packed

Garlic, 1 clove

Lemon zest, finely grated, 1 tablespoon

Sea salt

Extra-virgin olive oil

MAKES 4 SERVINGS

1. In a large pot, combine the carrots, onion, garlic, millet, and 2 cups (16 fl oz/475 ml) water. Bring to a boil over high heat, then reduce the heat to medium-low, cover, and cook until the vegetables and millet are very tender, about 30 minutes.

2. Transfer the carrot mixture to a blender and secure the lid. Hold the lid down with a folded kitchen towel and blend until smooth. Add the nondairy milk, thyme, ½ teaspoon salt, ¼ teaspoon pepper and blend until smooth. Transfer the soup to a medium pot and stir over medium-low heat just to heat through.

3. To make the gremolata, using a chef's knife, chop together the carrot tops and garlic until finely minced. Add the lemon zest and continue to mince. Transfer to a small bowl and add ¼ teaspoon salt and a drizzle of oil. Stir to mix.

4. Ladle the soup into bowls and top each with about 1 tablespoon gremolata. Serve right away.

THAI CORN & TOFU SOUP WITH CILANTRO

Coconut milk is the plant-based cook's secret weapon, delivering a creamy intensity straight from the can. Coconut can be grown on eco-friendly farms with little need for water or inputs. It works magic with tofu, and simmering the cubes in a savory-sweet-sour broth infuses them with Thai flavors. For a heartier meal, serve over cooked brown rice.

Coconut milk, 1 can
(13½ fl oz/400 ml)

Vegetable broth, 2 cups
(16 fl oz/475 ml)

Fresh ginger, 1-inch (2.5-cm) piece,
peeled and sliced

Lime zest, from 1 large lime,
pared in a wide strip

Vegan Thai green curry paste,
1 tablespoon, plus more to taste

Tamari, 1 tablespoon, plus more
to taste

Organic sugar, 1 teaspoon

Sea salt

Red chiles (such Red Fresno),
2 large, seeded and chopped

Corn on the cob, 2 ears, shucked
and kernels stripped

Carrot, 1 large, quartered
lengthwise and thinly sliced

Extra-firm tofu, 12 oz (340 g),
drained and cubed

Lime juice, 2 tablespoons

Fresh cilantro, ½ cup (¾ oz/20 g)
chopped, plus 4 sprigs

1. In a large pot, combine the coconut milk, broth, ginger, lime zest, curry paste, tamari, sugar, and ½ teaspoon salt. Bring to a boil over medium-high heat, then reduce the heat to low and simmer until the flavors are melded, about 10 minutes. Add the chiles, corn kernels, carrot, and tofu and simmer until the carrots are tender, about 10 minutes. Stir in the lime juice and taste for seasoning; if desired, add more curry paste, tamari, or salt. Remove the ginger slices and lime zest before serving; if you are making the soup to eat the next day, leave them in to infuse overnight.

2. Ladle the soup into bowls and sprinkle with the chopped cilantro. Garnish each with a cilantro sprig and serve right away.

MAKES 4 SERVINGS

COCONUT-CURRY
BUTTERNUT SQUASH SOUP

At once fragrant, sweet, and spicy, this soup makes the most of the fall squash harvest, and the bright orange flesh gives your immune system a powerful beta-carotene boost. Coconut milk adds creamy richness without any dairy and effortlessly creates an intoxicating appeal. Garnish the bowls of soup with the leaves and purple flowers of Thai basil, if you like.

Butternut squash, 1 large
(about 4 lb/1.8 kg)

Olive oil, 1½ tablespoons

Shallots, 4 large (about 3 oz/90 g total), thinly sliced

Fresh ginger, 1 tablespoon peeled and grated

Garlic, 1 clove, minced

Vegetable broth, 3 cups
(24 fl oz/700 ml)

Sea salt

Vegan Thai red curry paste,
1 teaspoon

Coconut milk, ¾ cup
(6 fl oz/180 ml)

Lime juice, 2 teaspoons

MAKES 4 SERVINGS

1. Using a sharp, heavy knife, trim the stem end from the squash, then cut in half lengthwise. Scoop out the seeds and discard. Peel each half and then cut the flesh into 1-inch (2.5-cm) cubes.

2. In a large pot, warm the oil over medium heat. Add the shallots and cook, stirring occasionally, until until softened, 2–3 minutes. Add the ginger and garlic and cook, stirring, until fragrant but not browned, about 1 minute. Add the squash, broth, and ½ teaspoon salt. Bring to a boil over high heat, then reduce the heat to maintain a simmer, cover, and cook until the squash is tender when pierced with a fork, about 20 minutes. Remove from the heat and let cool slightly.

3. In a small bowl, whisk together the curry paste and coconut milk until well blended. In a blender or food processor, working in batches if necessary, blend the soup until smooth. Return to the pot and stir in the curry–coconut milk mixture. Reheat the soup gently over medium heat just until hot. Season to taste with lime juice and salt.

4. Ladle the soup into bowls and serve right away.

CREMINI MUSHROOM & BARLEY SOUP WITH THYME

Thanks to widespread mushroom cultivation, you probably have a fungi farmer nearby, reducing the carbon footprint of your purchase. Many mushroom cultivators grow their crop on sterilized leftovers, making use of spent grain from breweries, almond husks, corncobs, sawdust, and other organic waste materials. The recipe also includes barley, a staple since around 11,000 years ago. This sustainable grain grows easily in poor soils with little water, even at high altitudes.

Dried mushrooms (any kind),
2 oz (60 g)

Bay leaves, 2

Fresh thyme, 1 sprig, plus 1
tablespoon leaves

Black peppercorns, 1 teaspoon

Yellow onion, 1 large

Celery, 1 rib

Carrot, 1 large

Garlic, 2 cloves

Olive oil, 2 tablespoons

Pearled barley, ½ cup
(3½ oz/100 g)

Sherry, ½ cup (4 fl oz/120 ml)

Tamari, ⅓ cup (2¾ fl oz/80 ml)

Sea salt

Cremini or button mushrooms,
1 lb (450 g) sliced

Freshly ground pepper

MAKES 8 SERVINGS

1. In a large pot, combine 10 cups (80 fl oz/2.4 l) water, the dried mushrooms, bay leaves, thyme sprig, and peppercorns and place over high heat. While the water heats up, chop the onion and celery, peel and chop the carrot, and add the trims and peels to the pot, reserving the chopped vegetables. Peel and chop the garlic and add the peels to the pot, reserving the chopped garlic. Bring the water just to a boil, then reduce the heat to maintain a gentle simmer, keeping the heat low so the stock doesn't boil, which would make it turn bitter. Cover and cook for 40 minutes. Strain the stock, then return the liquid to the pot. Add water, if needed, to make 8 cups (64 fl oz/1.9 l).

2. In another large pot, warm the oil over medium heat. Add the reserved chopped onion, celery, carrot, garlic, and thyme leaves and cook, stirring occasionally, until the vegetables are softened, about 10 minutes. Sauté until softened, about 10 minutes. Add the barley, 8 cups stock (from step 1), the sherry, tamari, and ½ teaspoon salt. Bring to a boil over high heat, then reduce the heat to maintain a simmer, cover, and cook until the barley is tender, about 25 minutes. Add the fresh mushrooms and simmer until softenened, 4–5 minutes. Season to taste with salt and pepper.

3. Ladle the soup into bowls and serve right away.

BLACK BEAN–BUTTERNUT CHILI WITH MASA DUMPLINGS

Instead of serving chili with corn bread or tortilla chips, simmer small masa dumplings right in the bubbly stew. Masa is a form of cornmeal that has undergone nixtamalization, a treatment using lime to soften the grain, which adds calcium and makes other nutrients more absorbable. Diced winter squash and red bell pepper add pops of color and veggie goodness. This recipe calls for canned beans, but if you prefer, soak and cook ½ cup (3½ oz/100 g) dried black beans ahead of time to substitute.

Extra-virgin olive oil, 1 tablespoon

Yellow onion, 1½ cups (7½ oz/210 g) finely chopped

Red bell pepper, 1, seeded and finely chopped

Garlic, 1 tablespoon finely chopped

Chili powder, 1 tablespoon

Ground cumin, 1 teaspoon

Ground cloves, ⅛ teaspoon

Vegetable broth, 2 cups (16 fl oz/475 ml)

Diced fire-roasted tomatoes, 1 can (15 oz/425 g)

Butternut squash, 1 cup (8 oz/225 g) cubed (½-inch/12-mm cubes)

Bay leaf, 1

Masa Dumpling Dough (page 160)

Black beans, 1 can (15 oz/425 g), drained and rinsed

Sea salt and freshly ground pepper

MAKES 4 SERVINGS

1. In a large pot, warm the oil over medium heat. Add the onion and bell pepper and cook, stirring occasionally, until the onion is translucent, about 5 minutes. Add the garlic, chili powder, cumin, and cloves and cook, stirring occasionally, until aromatic, about 1 minute. Add the broth, tomatoes, squash, and bay leaf and bring to a simmer. Reduce the heat to maintain a simmer, cover, and cook until the squash is tender, about 15 minutes.

2. Meanwhile, make the masa dumpling dough. Gently form the dumpling mixture into 1-inch (2.5-cm) balls.

3. Uncover the chili, add the beans, and season to taste with salt and pepper. Drop the dumplings into the soup, pushing them down into the liquid until they are half submerged. Cover and simmer until the dumplings are puffy and cooked through, about 8 minutes. To test for doneness, remove a dumpling from the soup and cut it in half. It should be dry and fluffy in the center. If not, cover and continue to cook for a few more minutes.

4. Ladle the chili and dumplings into deep bowls and serve right away.

LENTIL-MISO SOUP WITH SPINACH

Easy to find and inexpensive, lentils are the plant-based eater's friend, delivering protein, fiber, and minerals in comforting soups like this one. Instead of using a meat-based stock, you'll add umami and depth to the soup with miso, a Japanese condiment made of fermented soybeans and sometimes other beans and grains.

Dried green lentils, 1 cup
(7 oz/200 g), sorted and rinsed

Celery, 1 rib, chopped

Carrot, 1 large, chopped

Cabbage, 2 cups (6 oz/170 g)
chopped

Fresh ginger, 2 tablespoons peeled
and chopped

Red pepper flakes, ½ teaspoon

Red or white miso, ¼ cup
(2 oz/60 g)

Baby spinach, 2 cups (4 oz/120 g)
chopped

MAKES 4 SERVINGS

1. In a large pot, combine the lentils and 6 cups (48 fl oz/1.4 l) water and place over medium-high heat. Add the celery, carrot, cabbage, ginger, and red pepper flakes as the water comes to a boil. Once it is boiling, cover and reduce the heat to medium-low. Cook, stirring occasionally, until the lentils are tender and starting to fall apart, about 1 hour. Uncover and add a little water if the soup is too thick.

2. In a small bowl, mash the miso with ¼ cup (2 fl oz/60 ml) water to make a smooth paste. Stir the miso mixture into the lentils, add the spinach, and stir just until the soup is heated through and the spinach is wilted, 3–5 minutes.

3. Ladle the soup into bowls and serve right away.

TUSCAN-STYLE BEAN & KALE SOUP

This rustic soup is packed with super-healthy ingredients. Dried beans are a cornerstone of a sustainable diet. They are a high-protein food that is easy to grow and, once dried, requires no refrigeration or excess packaging. The soup tastes even better when made a day ahead. If you have leftovers, on the second day, do as the Italians do and ladle the reheated soup into bowls over a thick slice of stale whole-grain bread.

Dried borlotti or cranberry beans, 1 cup (7 oz/200 g)

Tuscan kale, 1 bunch (½ lb/225 g)

Olive oil, 2 tablespoons

Yellow onion, 1 large, chopped

Carrot, 1 large, peeled and chopped

Celery, 1 rib, thinly sliced

Garlic, 2 cloves, minced

Whole peeled tomatoes, 1 can (28 oz/800 g)

Bay leaf, 1

Red pepper flakes

Sea salt and freshly ground pepper

MAKES 8 SERVINGS

1. Pick over the beans for stones or broken or misshapen beans. Rinse thoroughly under cold running water and drain. Put the beans in a bowl and add fresh water to cover by 3–4 inches (7.5–10 cm). Let soak for at least 4 hours or up to overnight.

2. Drain the beans and transfer them to a large pot. Add water to cover the beans generously. Bring to a boil over high heat, reduce the heat to low, cover partially, and simmer gently until the beans are tender, 1–1½ hours, depending on their freshness. Drain the beans, pouring their liquid into another pot or a heatproof bowl. Set aside the beans and liquid separately.

3. Cut the stems and ribs from the kale leaves and discard. Stack the leaves, roll them up lengthwise, and cut crosswise into strips about ½ inch (12 mm) wide.

4. In a soup pot, warm the oil over medium-high heat. Add the onion, carrot, kale, and celery and sauté until the onion is translucent, 5–7. Add the garlic and cook until fragrant, about 1 minute. Pour the tomatoes into a bowl and, using your hands, crush them into small pieces. Add the tomatoes and their juices to the pot and stir to combine.

5. Measure the bean-cooking liquid and add water as needed to total 4 cups (32 fl oz/950 ml). Add the beans and the cooking-liquid mixture to the pot along with the bay leaf and a pinch of red pepper flakes. Bring to a boil over medium-high heat, reduce the heat to medium-low, cover, and simmer just until the beans are heated through, about 10 minutes. Season to taste with salt and pepper.

6. Ladle the soup into bowls and serve right away.

CELERY ROOT BISQUE

This silky soup tastes creamy without a drop of dairy because the starch in the root vegetables thickens the broth and imparts its dreamy texture. Root vegetables are a low-impact crop and thanks to modern storage techniques, the fall harvest holds its nutrients all winter. Serve with warm whole-grain bread to mop up every last drop of soup.

Extra-virgin olive oil, 1 tablespoon

Yellow onion, 1½ cups (7½ oz/210 g) finely chopped

Parsnip, 1, peeled and cut into ½-inch (12-mm) pieces

Celery, 1 rib, thinly sliced

Garlic, 2 teaspoons finely chopped

Vegetable broth, 3 cups (24 fl oz/700 ml)

Celery root, 1 (about 14 oz/400 g), peeled and cut into ½-inch (12-mm) pieces

Yukon gold potato, 1 large (½ lb/225 g), peeled and cut into ½-inch (12-mm) pieces

Dried savory or thyme, 1 teaspoon

Ground nutmeg, ¼ teaspoon

Sea salt and freshly ground pepper

Fresh chives, 1 tablespoon finely chopped (optional)

MAKES 4 SERVINGS

1. In a large pot, warm the oil over medium heat. Add the onion, parsnip, and celery and cook, stirring occasionally, until the onion is translucent, about 5 minutes. Add the garlic and cook, stirring, until fragrant, about 30 seconds. Add the broth, celery root, potato, savory, and 2 cups (16 fl oz/475 ml) water. Bring to a boil over medium-high heat, then reduce the heat to low, cover, and simmer gently until the vegetables fall apart when pressed against the side of the pot, about 25 minutes.

2. Using an immersion blender, purée the soup until smooth. (Alternatively, using a blender, blend the soup in batches, holding the lid down with a folded kitchen towel. Pour the soup back into the pot.) Over low heat, stir in the nutmeg and season to taste with salt and pepper.

3. Ladle the soup into bowls. Garnish with the chives (if using) and serve right away.

Recipe note

Look for a celery root that has been trimmed of its diminutive stalks and leaves and has no mushy spots. To peel, start with a sharp vegetable peeler and then use a paring knife to cut out any crevices where dirt may be wedged.

TOFU-KIMCHI SOUP

Korean food is known for its use of fermented vegetables, especially kimchi, a simple mix of cabbage, chiles, and carrots that transforms any dish with its potent tangy, spicy flavors. This soup stars napa cabbage kimchi alongside soft tofu and zucchini. You can tame the spiciness of the soup by using mild kimchi and less chile paste, if desired.

Avocado oil, coconut oil, or peanut oil, 1 tablespoon

Yellow onion, ½, thinly sliced

Napa cabbage kimchi, 1 cup (3 oz/90 g) roughly chopped, plus ½ cup (4 fl oz/120 ml) juice from the kimchi jar

Garlic, 2 teaspoons finely chopped

Fresh ginger, 2 teaspoons peeled and finely chopped

Vegetable broth, 2 cups (16 fl oz/475 ml)

Mirin, ¼ cup (2 fl oz/60 ml)

Zucchini, 1 small, halved lengthwise and sliced into ¼-inch (6-mm) pieces

Gochujang or sambal oelek, 1–2 tablespoons (optional)

Organic sugar, 1 teaspoon

Soft tofu, ½ lb (225 g)

Soy sauce or tamari, 1–2 tablespoons

Toasted sesame oil, 1 teaspoon

Green onions, white and pale green parts, 3 tablespoons thinly sliced

MAKES 4 SERVINGS

1. In a large pot, warm the avocado oil over medium heat. Add the onion and cook, stirring occasionally, until it begins to brown, about 4 minutes. Add the chopped kimchi, garlic, and ginger, and cook, stirring occasionally, until fragrant, about 2 minutes.

2. Add the broth, reserved kimchi juice, mirin, zucchini, gochujang to taste (if using), sugar, and 2 cups (16 fl oz/475 ml) water and bring to a simmer. Cover and cook until the zucchini is tender, about 10 minutes. Break up the tofu into 1-inch (2.5-cm) pieces and gently stir it into the soup. Cook until heated through, about 5 minutes.

3. Taste the broth—it should be spicy, sweet, and a little sour from the kimchi. Adjust the seasoning to taste with soy sauce and more gochujang, if desired. Stir in the sesame oil.

4. Ladle the soup into bowls. Sprinkle with the green onions and serve right away.

Recipe note

Gochujang is a spicy-sweet red condiment made from red chiles and fermented beans. The thick paste is used extensively in Korean cuisine as a complement for everything from soup to grilled tofu.

THE POWER OF ROOTS & SHOOTS

The Jane Goodall Institute's global youth empowerment program, known as Roots & Shoots, began in 1991. A group of 12 Tanzanian teenagers met with Jane Goodall, after hearing her speak at their school, to discuss local environmental issues. Concerned about dynamite fishing—which involves tossing explosives into the water to kill fish for easy collection—and the export of live birds, they felt hopeless and distressed.

Inspired by their compassion and energy, Jane realized the solution was right in front of them—their ability to create change. Roots & Shoots was born with the goal to inspire young people of all ages to understand their ability to create meaningful change in their communities through projects for people, other animals, and the environment. The beauty of Roots & Shoots is that the model helps young people understand issues holistically, very much like Jane did thinking through animal-agriculture, in order to see a problem from all sides and develop community-based solutions. Roots & Shoots projects range from helping their schools use reusable bags, community gardens to improve healthy food access, and organized trash cleanups. Others focus on bettering the quality of life for all humans, including closing educational inequality gaps in science, technology, and mathematics, and fostering connections between seniors living in elder care facilities and youth. Service projects for animals have involved kids reading to shelter dogs to improve literacy, planting trees to restore habitats, and organizing fundraisers for displaced animals affected by wildfires. Roots & Shoots encourages young activists to *look at the world around them and design service projects that bring about local change, inspiring them to be the change they wish to see in their communities.*

Like the magic and power of seeds, Roots & Shoots provides opportunities worldwide to build a powerful network of changemakers seeking to live in harmony with the planet. Since its creation, this powerful program has reached hundreds of thousands of young people in countries around the globe. Most of all, young people in Roots & Shoots, from elementary school through university and beyond, develop compassionate traits—empathy, critical thinking, inspiring their peers, and more—through these projects; skills that will help them to build a better world for all.

Of the original 12 students, one went on to serve as the minister of the environment for Tanzania, another became the Roots & Shoots' national director in Tanzania, and many others pursued careers in journalism, sciences, education, and beyond.

"Every time I explain to an audience the symbolism that led to naming our youth program 'Roots & Shoots,' I describe the magic, the life force within a seed that is so powerful that tiny roots, in order to reach the water, can work their way through rocks, and the tiny shoot, in order to reach the sun, can find a way through crevices in a brick wall. And, in the end, the rocks and walls—symbolizing all the harm we have inflicted on the planet—will be pushed aside and cast down.

The power is illustrated all around us—even in the middle of a city, seeds that have ended up in cracks between the paving stones will push out that tentative shoot, and down below, the roots move slowly, unseen beneath the concrete. Roots & Shoots—the strength of the youth of the world." [1]

Learn more about Roots & Shoots and join for free at rootsandshoots.org. Follow us **@rootsandshoots.**

---

[1] Goodall and Hudson, *Seeds of Hope*, 118–119.

SIDES & SALADS

"It is not too late to change direction. We can once again become connected with the food we eat, and learn to understand its nature and its history and embrace a more natural diet."—Jane

STRAWBERRY, ASPARAGUS & BIBB LETTUCE SALAD WITH WHITE BEANS

Strawberries and asparagus are part of the glory of spring and reach their peak freshness and flavor at the same time. Here, asparagus spears are arranged so as to "frame" the reds and pinks of the bright berries, making this a gorgeous salad that's fit for company. Both asparagus and strawberries are perennial plants, saving the farmer the energy and resources of replanting every year.

FOR THE DRESSING

Shallot, 1 small, peeled

Strawberries, 4 small, hulled

Balsamic vinegar, 2 tablespoons

Organic sugar, ½ teaspoon

Sea salt

Extra-virgin olive oil, ¼ cup
(2 fl oz/60 ml)

Asparagus, 16 spears, tough ends snapped off

Cooked white beans, 1½ cups
(10½ oz/300 g) drained

Bibb lettuce, 1 large head

Strawberries, 1 lb (18 oz/450 g), hulled and halved or quartered

MAKES 4 SERVINGS

1. To make the dressing, in a food processor or blender, mince the shallot. Add the 4 small strawberries and process until chopped. Add the vinegar, sugar, and ½ teaspoon salt and process until blended. With the machine running, drizzle in the oil and process until smooth. Set aside.

2. Bring a large pot of water to a boil and add 1 teaspoon salt. Add the asparagus and cook until tender-crisp, about 30 seconds. Drain, rinse with cold water, and refrigerate until serving time. Place the white beans in a medium bowl and drizzle with half of the dressing. Toss gently to coat.

3. When ready to serve, on each of 4 salad plates, arrange 4 spears of asparagus on the side. Place a few lettuce leaves in the center of the plate. Pile the beans in the lettuce cups and arrange the quartered strawberries all around. Drizzle with the remaining dressing and serve right away.

SOBA NOODLE SALAD WITH EDAMAME & WASABI PEAS

Edamame is a variety of soybean that has been bred for a sweet, buttery flavor and is picked while immature and green. Buy organic edamame, preferably grown near you, for the most environmentally friendly meal. In this dish, buckwheat noodles made from high-mineral, sustainable buckwheat flour, provide a satisfyingly slippery bases.

FOR THE MISO DRESSING

Apple cider vinegar, ¼ cup
(2 fl oz/60 ml)

Olive oil, 2 tablespoons

White miso, 2 tablespoons

Agave nectar, 1 tablespoon

Fresh ginger, 2 teaspoons peeled and grated

Wasabi paste, 1 teaspoon

Sea salt

Shelled edamame, 2 cups
(12 oz/340 g), thawed

Green tea or regular soba noodles,
½ lb (225 g)

Ripe avocado, 1 large, pitted, peeled, and cubed

Fresh cilantro leaves, ½ cup
(½ oz/15 g) packed

Green onions, 2, thinly sliced

Wasabi peas, ½ cup (2½ oz/70 g)

MAKES 4 SERVINGS

1. To make the miso dressing, combine all of the ingredients except salt in a screw-top jar and shake well. Season to taste with salt.

2. Bring a saucepan of water to a boil over medium-high heat. Add the edamame and cook until just tender, about 2 minutes. Remove with a slotted spoon. Rinse under cold water and drain. Add the noodles to the same pan of boiling water and cook until just tender, about 4 minutes. Drain.

3. Place the noodles and edamame in a large bowl. Add the avocado, cilantro, green onions, half of the wasabi peas, and the dressing. Toss gently to combine. Top with the remaining wasabi peas and serve right away.

Recipe note

This recipe uses premixed wasabi paste in a tube, which is milder than powdered or fresh wasabi. Assemble this salad just before serving to ensure the wasabi peas retain their crunch.

GRILLED SQUASH & ORZO
SALAD WITH PINE NUTS

Fire up the grill to make the most of seasonal summer squashes, which taste best with a kiss of smoke and sear. Look for the smallest ones you can find, and if you see some pattypans or unusual varieties of zucchini, try them grilled—you'll love them. A grill basket can be very helpful for this dish, to prevent the squash slices from dropping into the fire. Use whole-grain orzo if you can find it.

Mixed yellow squash and
zucchini, 2 lb (1 kg)

Olive oil, 1½ tablespoons

Sea salt and freshly ground pepper

Orzo, ½ lb (225 g)

Pine nuts, ½ cup (2½ oz/70 g)

Lemon juice, 3 tablespoons

Apple cider vinegar, 1 tablespoon

Fresh mint, 3 tablespoons chopped

MAKES 4 SERVINGS

1. Trim and cut the squash lengthwise into slices ¼ inch (6 mm) thick. Place in a bowl and add ½ tablespoon of the oil, ½ teaspoon salt, and a few grinds of pepper. Toss to coat.

2. Prepare a charcoal or gas grill for direct-heat cooking over medium-high heat. Grill the squash, turning once, until tender, 5–8 minutes total. Let cool and cut into 1½-inch (4-cm) pieces. Transfer to a large bowl.

3. Bring a pot of salted water to a boil. Add the orzo and cook until al dente according to package instructions. Drain and rinse under cold running water.

4. Meanwhile, in a frying pan, toast the pine nuts over medium-low heat, stirring, until fragrant and starting to brown, about 4 minutes. Transfer to a plate to cool.

5. Add the orzo to the bowl with the squash along with the remaining 1 tablespoon oil, the lemon juice, vinegar, and pine nuts and toss to combine. Season to taste with salt and pepper. Garnish with the mint and serve right away.

NEW POTATO & RADISH SALAD WITH MUSTARD-DILL VINAIGRETTE

Tart, salty, and full of pickled flavor, cornichons are a smart way to keep vegetables in the pantry. Along with mustard, they add zip to the tender waxy potatoes and crunchy radishes and celery in this salad. If your radish leaves are fresh and green, chop them and toss into the salad as well to add nutrients and prevent food waste.

FOR THE VINAIGRETTE

Apple cider vinegar, 6 tablespoons (3 fl oz/90 ml)

Cornichons, 7, minced

Fresh dill, ¼ cup (⅓ oz/10 g) minced

Shallot, 1, minced

Vegan mustard, 3 tablespoons

Organic sugar, 1 tablespoon

Sea salt

Extra-virgin olive oil, ½ cup (4 fl oz/120 ml) plus 1 tablespoon

Red new potatoes, 2 lb (1 kg)

Sea salt

Celery, 4 ribs, finely chopped

Radishes, 8 large, trimmed and finely chopped

Fresh dill, 2 tablespoons coarsely chopped

MAKES 6 SERVINGS

1. To make the vinaigrette, in a large bowl, whisk together the vinegar, cornichons, minced dill, shallot, mustard, sugar, and ½ teaspoon salt until the sugar and salt dissolve. Add the oil in a thin stream, whisking constantly until the vinaigrette is well blended. Season to taste with salt.

2. Have ready a bowl of ice water. In a large saucepan, combine the potatoes, 1 tablespoon salt, and water to cover by 1 inch (2.5 cm), and bring to a boil over high heat. Reduce the heat to medium, cover partially, and simmer until the potatoes are just tender when pierced with a paring knife, about 10 minutes.

3. Drain the potatoes in a colander and then plunge them into the ice water. Let cool, then drain again and pat dry. Cut each potato into halves or quarters.

4. Whisk the vinaigrette to recombine, then add the potatoes to the bowl. Add the celery and radishes and toss gently. Season to taste with salt. Sprinkle the salad with the chopped dill and serve right away.

ROASTED ASPARAGUS &
GREEN ONIONS WITH ROMESCO

In Spain, the seasonal arrival of a certain chile pepper or mushroom is often marked with a food festival. The *calçot* is a type of green onion that grows in the northern Spanish region of Catalonia. It's served grilled with romesco—a kind of pesto made with roasted bell peppers and almonds—at an annual festival called *Calçotada*. Here, use the freshest green onions for your at-home fiesta.

FOR THE ROMESCO

Red bell peppers, 2 large, or 1 jar (12 oz/340 g) roasted peppers

Extra-virgin olive oil, ¼ cup (2 fl oz/60 ml)

Garlic, 8 cloves, coarsely chopped

Sliced almonds, ½ cup (2 oz/60 g), toasted

Tomato, 1 large, chopped

Sea salt

Asparagus, 1 lb (450 g), tough ends snapped off

Green onions, 1 bunch

Extra-virgin olive oil

MAKES 4 SERVINGS

1. To make the romesco, place a rack in the top third of the oven and preheat the broiler.

2. Place the bell peppers on a small rimmed baking sheet and broil, turning occasionally, until the skins are charred on all sides, about 10 minutes. Transfer to a bowl, cover, and let steam for 15 minutes. Remove and let cool. Peel and discard the skins, stems, and seeds. Pat dry. Measure out 1½ cups (12/oz/340 g). (If using jarred peppers, drain, rinse, and pat dry.)

3. In a small sauté pan, warm the oil over medium heat. Add the garlic and cook, stirring frequently, until fragrant and lightly golden on the edges, about 1 minute. Remove from the heat.

4. In a food processor, combine the peppers, almonds, and tomato and process. Scrape down the sides of the bowl and repeat until smooth. Add the garlic-oil mixture and ½ teaspoon salt and process until smooth. Transfer to a medium bowl.

5. In a bowl, toss the asparagus spears and green onions with oil to coat. On a grill or under a hot broiler, grill or broil the vegetables, turning once, until slightly shriveled but still firm enough to eat with fingers, about 5 minutes. Place on a platter and serve right away with the romesco for dipping.

BABY GREENS SAUTÉED WITH PINE NUTS

We all need to eat more greens. Packed with vitamins, minerals, antioxidants, and fiber, leafy greens are some of the most nutrient-dense foods on earth, offering plant-based diners impressive amounts of calcium and iron. In the Mediterranean style, serve yours sautéed in extra-virgin olive oil, with garlic and some crunchy nuts to contrast with the greens' silkiness.

Baby braising greens, 1 lb (450 g), or baby spinach, 12 oz (340 g)

Extra-virgin olive oil, 2 tablespoons

Red onion, 1, sliced

Garlic, 3 cloves, coarsely chopped

Golden raisins, ¼ cup (1½ oz/40 g)

Pine nuts or raw sunflower seeds, 2 tablespoons

Sea salt

MAKES 4–6 SERVINGS

1. Wash the greens and dry them in a salad spinner or on towels. In a large frying pan, warm the oil over medium-high heat. Add the onion and cook, stirring often, until softened and slightly browned, about 4 minutes.

2. Add the greens, garlic, raisins, pine nuts, and ½ teaspoon salt and cook, turning the greens until they are evenly wilted and deep green, about 3 minutes. Serve right away.

PAN-SEARED CAULIFLOWER
WITH GARLIC & CAPERS

Cauliflower is part of the Brassica family, which also includes cabbage, broccoli, and kale. The vegetables are rich in sulforaphane, a plant chemical that is believed to have powerful health benefits. Cauliflower is a chameleon of sorts, depending on how you cook it, becoming deep and intense when seared and mild when boiled. Here you'll blanch it to tenderize the sturdy florets, then sear it until the edges are nicely browned, for an intense flavor.

Cauliflower, 1 medium head,
1¼ lb (570 g)

Carrot, 1 large

Olive oil, ¼ cup (2 fl oz/60 ml)

Garlic, 4 cloves, minced

Capers, 2 tablespoons, rinsed
and drained

Red pepper flakes, ½ teaspoon

Sea salt and freshly ground pepper

MAKES 4 SERVINGS

1. Trim the cauliflower and cut into 2-inch (5-cm) florets (you should have about 4 cups/8 oz/225 g). Cut the carrot into diagonal slices. Bring a large pot of water to a boil over high heat. Add the vegetables, stir, and cook until tender-crisp, about 1 minute. Drain and let cool.

2. In a large frying pan, warm the oil over medium-high heat. Add the cauliflower and carrot and cook, stirring, until starting to soften, about 3 minutes. Add the garlic, capers, and red pepper flakes and cook, stirring, until the vegetables are browned, about 3 minutes. Season to taste with salt and pepper and serve right away.

BULGUR SALAD WITH PEPPERS, CHICKPEAS & PISTACHIOS

Roasted peppers and dried fruit add bursts of color and sweetness to this whole-grain salad, while toasted pistachios lend crunch. Bulgur is a form of wheat that has been steamed and dried, so it cooks quickly on the stovetop or simply by soaking in hot broth. Pomegranate molasses is pomegranate juice that has been boiled until thick and syrupy.

Medium-grind bulgur, 1½ cups
(9 oz/250 g)

Vegetable broth, 2¼ cups
(18 fl oz/525 ml)

Lemon juice, ¼ cup (2 fl oz/60 ml)

Pomegranate molasses, ¼ cup
(2¾ oz/80 g)

Organic sugar, 2 teaspoons

Sea salt and freshly ground pepper

Extra-virgin olive oil, 6 tablespoons
(3 fl oz/90 ml)

Chickpeas, 1 can (15 oz/425 g),
drained and rinsed

Red bell peppers, 2 large

Roasted pistachios, ¾ cup
(3 oz/90 g)

Fresh flat-leaf parsley or cilantro,
½ cup (¾ oz/20 g) chopped

Dried tart cherries, 1 cup
(6 oz/170 g), roughly chopped

MAKES 6 SERVINGS

1. Put the bulgur in a large heatproof bowl. In a small saucepan, bring the broth to a boil. Pour the boiling broth over the bulgur, cover, and let stand until the liquid has been absorbed, about 30 minutes.

2. In a small nonreactive bowl, whisk together the lemon juice, pomegranate molasses, sugar, 1½ teaspoons salt, and several grinds of pepper until the sugar and salt dissolve. Slowly whisk in the oil to make a dressing. Season to taste with salt and pepper.

3. In a small bowl, stir together the chickpeas and ½ teaspoon salt. Whisk the dressing to recombine, then add it, along with the chickpeas, to the bowl with the bulgur. Stir to mix well. Cover and refrigerate for 2 hours.

4. Meanwhile, place a rack in the top third of the oven and preheat the broiler.

5. Place the bell peppers on a small rimmed baking sheet and broil, turning occasionally, until the skins are charred on all sides, about 10 minutes. Transfer to a bowl, cover, and let steam for 15 minutes. Remove and let cool. Peel and discard the skins, stems, and seeds, and cut the flesh into small dice.

6. When ready to serve, in a small bowl, stir together the pistachios and a pinch of salt. Add the pistachios, roasted peppers, parsley, and dried cherries to the bulgur and toss to mix well. Season to taste with salt and pepper. Divide the salad among bowls and serve right away.

CARROT, OLIVE & ALMOND SALAD

Carrots are full of antioxidants and so are plump olives, a star of the healthy Mediterranean diet. If shaving the carrots lengthwise seems too labor intensive or difficult, you can shave or thinly slice them into coins. Meaty green olives are delicious in this salad, although any olives, including oil-cured black ones, will impart a pleasant briny and salty note to the mix.

Cumin seeds, ½ teaspoon

Multicolored carrots, 1 lb (450 g)

Green olives, pitted, ¼ cup
(1½ oz/40 g)

Fresh flat-leaf parsley, ¼ cup
(¼ oz/7 g) loosely packed

Lemon juice, 1 teaspoon

Extra-virgin olive oil, 2 tablespoons

Sea salt and freshly ground pepper

Roasted almonds, ¼ cup
(1¼ oz/35 g) chopped

MAKES 4 SERVINGS

1. In a frying pan, toast the cumin seeds over medium-low heat, stirring, until fragrant and starting to brown, 2–3 minutes. Transfer to a plate and let cool.

2. Using a mandoline or a box grater, shave the carrots lengthwise into thin ribbons. Transfer to a large bowl and set aside.

3. Coarsely chop the olives and parsley. Transfer to a small bowl, add the lemon juice and toasted cumin seeds, and stir with a fork to combine. Add the oil in a thin stream, whisking until the dressing is well blended. Season to taste with salt and pepper.

4. Add the dressing to the carrots and toss well. Divide the salad among plates, sprinkle with the almonds, and serve right away.

KALE WITH PARSLEY-WALNUT PESTO & ROASTED PEPPERS

Why massage your kale? The sturdy leaves can be a bit challenging to chew when raw unless you take a couple of minutes to rub them to a silkier texture. Adding a lemony pesto to the slivered leaves, then giving them a good rubdown, makes the nutrient-dense, sustainable green a delight to eat.

Fresh flat-leaf parsley leaves, 2 cups (2 oz/60 g)

Walnuts, ¼ cup (1 oz/30 g)

Garlic, 1 clove

Extra-virgin olive oil, ¼ cup (2 fl oz/60 ml)

Lemon juice, 2 tablespoons

Sea salt

Lacinato kale, 1 bunch

Yukon gold potato, 1 large (about 9 oz/250 g), cubed and steamed

Jarred roasted red peppers, 1 cup (6 oz/170 g), drained, patted dry, and cut into strips

MAKES 4–6 SERVINGS

1. To make the parsley-walnut pesto, in a blender or food processor, combine the parsley, walnuts, and garlic and blend until minced. Add the oil, lemon juice, and 1 teaspoon salt and blend until smooth.

2. Rip the kale leaves from the stems and thinly slice the leaves. Thinly slice the thin upper half of the stems, discarding the thicker base of the stems.

3. Place the kale leaves and sliced stems in a large bowl, add the pesto, and massage the kale for about 2 minutes. Add the potato and red peppers and toss to mix. Refrigerate until serving. The salad can be stored, tightly covered in the refrigerator, for up to 3 days.

Recipe note

Highly nutritious and slightly nutty-sweet, kale is more than a pretty garnish or an overlooked side dish. As a member of the Brassica family, it is a cold-hardy crop best planted in autumn, when temperatures begin to drop, and it matures best in cold weather. But it's not only versatile in the garden, where it can be planted in traditional or raised beds. In the kitchen, kale makes an excellent addition to salads and casseroles.

WINTER GADO GADO
SALAD WITH PEANUT SAUCE

Gado gado is an Indonesian salad consisting of crisp raw cabbage and other vegetables, topped with tofu, boiled eggs, and a creamy peanut-coconut sauce. This version uses roasted root vegetables for an earthy seasonal twist—no need for eggs! Buy prebaked marinated tofu for a quick solution or use the baked tofu from Sesame Noodles with Green Beans & Tofu (page 107). This makes more peanut sauce than you'll need for the salad; store the leftover sauce in a jar in the fridge and drizzle it over vegetables, tofu, or rice.

Carrot, 1 large, thickly sliced

Turnip, 1, 8 oz (225 g), cubed

Sweet potato, 1, 8 oz (225 g), cut into wedges

Avocado oil, 1 tablespoon

Lime zest, grated, 2 teaspoons

FOR THE PEANUT SAUCE

Coconut milk, 1 can
(13½ fl oz/400 ml), unshaken

Red pepper flakes, to taste

Garlic, 2 large cloves, minced

Shallots, 5 small, minced

Smooth unsweetened peanut butter, 6 tablespoons (3½ oz/100 g)

Lime juice, 1 tablespoon

Organic sugar, 1 tablespoon

Sea salt

Napa cabbage, 4 cups
(12 oz/340 g) shredded

Prebaked or fried tofu, 1 lb
(450 g), cut into strips

MAKES 4 SERVINGS

1. Preheat the oven to 400°F (200°C).

   On a rimmed baking sheet, place the carrot, turnip, and sweet potato in three separate sections. Drizzle with the oil and sprinkle with the lime zest. Toss gently, keeping the vegetables separate. Cover the pan with foil or another pan that covers it completely and roast and roast until the vegetables are very tender when pierced with a paring knife, about 20 minutes. Let cool on a rack.

2. To make the peanut sauce, scoop the solidified part of the coconut milk into a small pot and place over medium heat. Add the red pepper flakes, garlic, and shallots and and cook, stirring occasionally, until the shallots are very soft, about 5 minutes.

3. Meanwhile, in a bowl, stir together the peanut butter, lime juice, and remaining coconut milk to make a smooth paste. When the shallots are tender, add the peanut butter mixture, sugar, and 1 teaspoon salt to the pot and stir to combine. Bring to a boil, then reduce the heat and simmer, stirring occasionally, until thickened slightly, about 2 minutes. Let cool.

4. To assemble the salad, place the cabbage on a large platter and arrange the roasted vegetables and tofu on top. Drizzle with some of the peanut sauce and serve right away, with more sauce on the side. The sauce can be stored, tightly covered in the refrigerator, for up to 2 days.

ROASTED SUMMER VEGGIE PENNE WITH CHICKPEAS

When the garden is in full swing, roast a panful of vegetables and toss with pasta for a simple plant-based comfort meal. The secret to enjoying pasta in a healthful way is to use whole-grain noodles and add more vegetables. If you haven't roasted fennel bulbs before, you're in for a treat; the oven brings out sweet and anise-y notes, giving the dish a lively boost. Nutritional yeast is the nondairy answer to a sprinkle of cheese and is a great source of vitamin B12.

Fennel bulb, 1, cut into ½-inch (12-mm) pieces, fronds reserved

Yellow squash, 1 large, quartered lengthwise and sliced crosswise

Red onion, 1, chopped

Garlic, 4 cloves, halved

Extra-virgin olive oil, ¼ cup (2 fl oz/60 ml)

Fresh thyme, 2 sprigs

Sea salt

Penne, ½ lb (225 g)

Roma tomatoes, 2 large, chopped

Kalamata olives, ¼ cup (1¼ oz/35 g), pitted and chopped

Chickpeas, 1 can (15 oz/425 g), drained and rinsed

Fresh basil leaves, ½ cup (1 oz/30 g), chopped

Nutritional yeast (optional)

MAKES 4–6 SERVINGS

1. Preheat the oven to 400°F (200°C). Have ready 2 rimmed baking sheets.

2. On 1 baking sheet, combine the chopped fennel, squash, onion, and garlic. Add 2 tablespoons of the oil and toss to coat. Add the thyme and ½ teaspoon salt and toss again. Transfer half of the mixture to the second baking sheet. Roast both pans for 15 minutes, then stir the vegetables. Reverse the position of the pans in the oven and roast until the vegetables are tender and lightly browned, about 15 minutes more. Cool on racks.

3. Meanwhile, bring a large pot of salted water to a boil. Add the penne and cook until al dente according to package instructions; drain. Chop enough of the reserved fennel fronds to measure about ½ cup (¾ oz/20 g).

4. In the empty pasta pot, combine the penne, roasted vegetables, tomatoes, olives, chickpeas, basil, fennel fronds, and the remaining 2 tablespoons oil. Toss to mix.

5. Divide the pasta and vegetables among bowls and serve right away, sprinkled with nutritional yeast, if desired.

BRUSSELS SPROUT & ARUGULA SALAD WITH WALNUTS

Walnut oil is a potent source of omega-3, the same beneficial fat found in salmon, so it's a great ingredient for a plant-based diet. The lush, nutty flavor of the oil will make a dish of plain steamed vegetables or a salad like this one really sing. Walnut oil is fragile, so once opened, keep it in the refrigerator and use it up within 4 months.

Brussels sprouts, 1 lb (450 g), trimmed

Walnuts, ½ cup (2 oz/60 g) chopped

Walnut oil, 1½ tablespoons

Apple cider vinegar, 1 tablespoon

Sea salt and freshly ground pepper

Arugula, 1 cup (1 oz/30 g)

MAKES 4 SERVINGS

1. Using a mandoline or a sharp knife, thinly shave the brussels sprouts lengthwise. Transfer to a bowl.

2. In a small frying pan, toast the walnuts over medium-low heat, stirring, until starting to brown, about 5 minutes. Let cool.

3. Add the oil and vinegar to the brussels sprouts and season to taste with salt and pepper. Toss to mix.

4. Divide the arugula among plates. Spoon the brussels sprouts and their dressing over the arugula, garnish with the walnuts, and serve right away.

ROASTED RATATOUILLE WITH BASIL

Eggplant is underappreciated, probably because it's often prepared poorly. It's really very easy to master, and preparing it is a snap. Roasting cubed eggplant with a medley of other vegetables ensures it will be cooked to melting tenderness and absorb the flavors around it. Ratatouille is a classic part of the healthful Mediterranean diet and can be enjoyed on its own, over toast or pasta, and even on pizza.

Eggplant, 1, 1 lb (450 g), cubed

Yellow onion, 1 large, chopped

Red bell pepper, 1, seeded and chopped

Zucchini, 1 large, 1 oz (310 g), quartered lengthwise and sliced crosswise

Tomatoes, 2 large, chopped

Garlic, 4 large cloves, halved

Dried thyme, 1 teaspoon

Sea salt

Extra-virgin olive oil, ¼ cup (2 fl oz/60 ml)

Fresh basil leaves, ½ cup (½ oz/15 g), shredded

MAKES 4 SERVINGS

1. Preheat the oven to 400°F (200°C).

2. In a large roasting pan, combine the eggplant, onion, bell pepper, zucchini, tomatoes, and garlic. Sprinkle with the thyme and ½ teaspoon salt, add the oil, and toss to coat. Cover the pan with foil or another pan that covers it completely.

3. Roast for about 20 minutes, then shake the pan and return to the oven for about 20 minutes more. Uncover, stir, and roast until the vegetables have browned slightly but are still juicy, about 20 minutes more. Stir the vegetables, scraping the bottom of the pan, and let cool.

4. Transfer the vegetables to a serving platter, garnish with the basil, and serve right away.

KALE & ROASTED SQUASH SALAD WITH MAPLE VINAIGRETTE

The fall farmers' market is a colorful sight, with orange, green, and yellow squashes piled alongside purple and green kale. Put both superfoods to good use in this salad, where slightly crunchy kale is studded with tender squash and drizzled with a tangy-sweet vinaigrette. This is one salad that is just as delicious the next day or even the day after that. Feel free to substitute any dried fruit for the raisins.

Acorn squash, 1 small, halved, seeded, and sliced

Sea salt

Brown sugar, 2 tablespoons

Paprika, ¼ teaspoon

Extra-virgin olive oil, 2 tablespoons plus 1 teaspoon

Raw pumpkin seeds (pepitas), ½ cup (2 oz/60 g)

Kale, 1 bunch, stems and ribs removed

Maple syrup, 2 tablespoons

Lemon juice, 2 tablespoons

Honeycrisp or other crisp, tart apple, 1 large, cored and chopped

Red onion, ¼ small, thinly sliced

Raisins or other chopped dried fruit, ½ cup (3 oz/90 g)

MAKES 4–6 SERVINGS

1. Preheat the oven to 400°F (200°C).

2. Lightly oil a rimmed baking sheet, place the squash on it, and season with salt. Roast for 20 minutes, then flip the slices and roast until tender and lightly browned, about 10 minutes more. Cool on a rack.

3. In a small bowl, stir together the brown sugar, paprika, and ½ teaspoon salt.

4. In a large sauté pan, warm 1 teaspoon of the oil over medium heat. Add the pumpkin seeds, stirring and swirling until they start to pop and smell toasty, 3–5 minutes. Add the brown sugar mixture and stir constantly until the sugar is melted and coats the seeds. Transfer to a medium bowl to cool.

5. Tear the kale leaves into bite-size pieces and place in a large bowl. In a small bowl, stir together the remaining 2 tablespoons oil, the maple syrup, lemon juice, and ½ teaspoon salt until well blended. Pour over the kale and massage the leaves for at least 2 minutes, until slightly softened.

6. Stir in the cooled squash, apple, onion, and raisins. Sprinkle with the spiced pumpkin seeds and serve right away.

WINTER SQUASH STUFFED WITH APPLES & WILD RICE

Sweet dumpling, delicata, and other small winter squashes make perfect vessels for stuffing. Wild rice, a traditional food of people like the Ojibwe communities of North America, has twice the protein of brown rice and abundant antioxidants to protect your health. It requires more liquid and a longer cooking time than white rice, but the result is a tender, chewy grain that pairs perfectly with countless vegetables and flavors.

Delicata or acorn squashes, 2 small, halved and seeded

Wild rice or brown rice, 1 cup (6 oz/185 g)

Extra-virgin olive oil, 1 tablespoon

Shallots, ½ cup (2 oz/60 g) chopped

Apples, 2 large, peeled, cored, and chopped into ½-inch (12-mm) pieces

Walnuts, 1 cup (4 oz/115 g) chopped

Dried sage, 2 teaspoons

Dried thyme, 1 teaspoon

Sea salt

MAKES 4 SERVINGS

Recipe note

These can be assembled in advance, tightly covered, and refrigerated for up to 3 days. To bake, let come to room temperature and bake at 400°F (200°C) for 30 minutes.

1. Preheat the oven to 400°F (200°C).

   Lightly oil a rimmed baking sheet and place the squash halves on it, cut side down. Roast until tender when pierced with a paring knife, about 20 minutes..

2. In a small pot, bring 2 cups (16 fl oz/475 ml) water to a boil. Add the rice and return to a boil. Reduce the heat to low, cover, and cook until tender, about 25 minutes for wild rice if hand harvested or 40–60 minutes if cultivated. (Brown rice should take about 40 minutes.) Remove from the heat and drain, if necessary. Set aside.

3. When the squashes are cool enough to handle, scoop out the flesh with a spoon, being careful not to tear the shell and leaving a thin layer of flesh all around the shell. Place the squash flesh in a large bowl and add the cooked rice.

4. In a large sauté pan, warm the oil over medium-high heat. Add the shallots and apples and and cook, stirring occasionally, until the shallots and the apples are soft and lightly browned, about 4 minutes. Add the walnuts, sage, thyme, and 1 teaspoon salt and stir briefly. Add the apple mixture to the bowl with the squash and rice and stir until well combined.

5. Stuff the squash shells with the rice mixture and place on the baking sheet. Roast until browned on top and heated through, about 20 minutes. Serve right away.

SWEET POTATO RISOTTO WITH WALNUTS

Arborio rice is easy to overcook when making risotto, whereas whole-grain rice is more forgiving. Thanks to the healthful bran layer on the grains, you can treat brown rice much more casually because it can't get mushy, and reheat it to your heart's content. A topping of walnuts on this sweet potato–infused risotto adds protein and omega-3 fats, as well as crunch and flavor.

Extra-virgin olive oil, 1 tablespoon

Yellow onion, 1, chopped

Sweet potato, 1, 9 oz (250 g), peeled and cut into small cubes

Brown rice or black rice, 1 cup (7 oz/250 g)

Vegan white wine, ½ cup (4 fl oz/120 ml)

Sea salt

Vegetable broth, 3 cups (24 fl oz/700 ml)

Dried thyme, 1 teaspoon

Nutritional yeast, 2 tablespoons

Fresh basil or flat-leaf parsley, ½ cup (¾ oz/20 g) chopped

Walnuts, ½ cup (2 oz/60 g) coarsely chopped

MAKES 4 SERVINGS

1. In a large sauté pan, warm the oil over medium-high heat. Add the onion and and sweet potato and cook, stirring occasionally and reducing the heat to low as it starts to sizzle, until the onion is translucent and the sweet potato starts to caramelize, 4–5 minutes. Add the rice and stir until it is hot to the touch. Add the wine and ½ teaspoon salt and stir until the pan is dry. Add the broth and thyme and bring to a boil over high heat. Cover, reduce the heat to medium-low, and cook until the rice and is tender, about 30 minutes.

2. Uncover the pan, stir, and test the grains; they should be tender and soupy. Raise the heat to a simmer to cook off the liquid, stirring to break the grains a little and make the risotto creamy. When the risotto is thickened, stir in the nutritional yeast and basil. Top with the walnuts and serve right away.

BULGUR & LENTIL PILAF WITH ALMONDS

Whole-grain bulgur and easy-to-cook lentils combine with aromatic vegetables, fragrant spices, and fresh herbs in a versatile side dish. Bulgur is made by parboiling wheat grains while still in the husk, then husking, drying, and chopping in varying sizes, from coarse to tiny. That process makes bulgur quicker to cook than other whole grains while preserving the protein, iron, and vitamin B6. Lentils provide plenty of protein, iron, and fiber. A topping of toasted almonds stands in for cheese or meat with plant-based crunch appeal to spare.

Dried brown lentils, ¾ cup
(5¼ oz/150 g)

Olive oil, 2 tablespoons

Yellow onion, 1, chopped

Garlic, 2 cloves, minced

Medium-grind bulgur, 1 cup
(6 oz/170 g)

Ground coriander, 1 teaspoon

Sea salt and freshly ground pepper

Vegetable broth or water, 2 cups
(16 fl oz/475 ml)

Fresh flat-leaf parsley, ⅓ cup
(⅓ oz/10 g)

Roasted almonds, ¼ cup
(1½ oz/45 g)

Lemon zest, finely grated,
1 tablespoon

Lemon juice, 2 tablespoons

MAKES 4 SERVINGS

1. Pick over the lentils for stones or grit. Rinse thoroughly under cold running water and drain. In a small saucepan, combine the lentils with water to cover by 2 inches (5 cm) and bring to a boil over medium-high heat. Reduce the heat to medium-low, cover, and simmer gently until the lentils are tender but firm to the bite, about 20 minutes. Drain well and set aside.

2. In a large frying pan, warm the oil over medium-high heat. Add the onion and cook, stirring often, until wilted, 2–3 minutes. Add the garlic, bulgur, coriander, and ¼ teaspoon each salt and pepper and cook, stirring often, until the garlic is fragrant, about 1 minute. Stir in the lentils and broth and bring to a boil. Reduce the heat to low, cover, and simmer until the bulgur starts to soften, about 5 minutes. Remove from the heat and let stand, covered, until the bulgur is tender, about 15 minutes.

3. Place the parsley, almonds, and lemon zest on a cutting board and coarsely chop them together. Fluff the lentil mixture with a fork and stir in the lemon juice. Season to taste with salt and pepper.

4. Mound the pilaf on a serving platter. Sprinkle with the almond mixture and serve right away.

CAULIFLOWER STEAKS
WITH CREAMY CURRY SAUCE

Cut "steaks" out of a head of cauliflower to show off the vegetable to its fullest. Searing and then roasting the thick slabs sweetens and concentrates their flavor, giving them universal appeal. Using the remaining stem and florets to make a creamy sauce prevents waste, and you should have plenty of sauce, perhaps even enough to serve over rice or vegetables the next day.

Cauliflower, 1 head (1½ lb/680 g)

Raw cashews, ½ cup (2½ oz/70 g), soaked overnight in cool water to cover by 1 inch (2.5 cm) and drained

Fresh ginger, 1 tablespoon peeled and chopped

Lemon zest, finely grated, 1 tablespoon

Sea salt

Ground cumin, 1 teaspoon

Ground turmeric, ¾ teaspoon

Ground coriander, ½ teaspoon

Cayenne pepper, ½ teaspoon

Coconut milk, 1 cup (8 fl oz/240 ml)

Avocado oil, 2 tablespoons

Cooked quinoa, rice, or millet, 1 cup (5 oz/140 g)

Toasted pistachios or cashews, chopped, for garnish

MAKES 2 SERVINGS

1. Trim the leaves from the cauliflower and partially trim the base. Stand the cauliflower up on the remaining base and cut out two 1-inch (2.5-cm) steaks from the center of the head. Set the steaks aside. Chop the remaining stem and florets into pieces 1 inch (2.5 cm) or smaller.

2. In a steamer basket set over simmering water, steam 4 cups (1 lb/400 g) of the chopped cauliflower until very soft, 15 minutes. (Reserve any extra chopped cauliflower for another use.)

3. Meanwhile, preheat the oven to 400°F (200°C). Have ready a rimmed baking sheet.

4. In a blender, combine the steamed cauliflower, cashews, ginger, and lemon zest and process until smooth, stopping to scrape down and repeating as needed. Add 1 teaspoon salt, the cumin, turmeric, coriander, and cayenne and process to blend. Add the coconut milk and process until very smooth. Transfer to a small pan and keep warm on the stove over very low heat.

5. In a large sauté pan, warm the oil over high heat. Carefully slide the cauliflower steaks into the oil and cook, turning once and pressing down with a sturdy spatula to make sure the cauliflower is in contact with the pan, until evenly browned, about 2 minutes per side. Transfer the steaks to the baking sheet and and roast until a paring knife inserted into the thick part of the stem meets no resistance, about 20 minutes.

6. To serve, spread half of the rice on each dinner plate. Ladle some sauce over it and place a cauliflower steak on top. Sprinkle with the nuts and serve right away.

SPINACH SALAD WITH ORANGES & ROASTED BEETS

Plump, sweet navel oranges are featured frequently in winter salads. They lend appealing color and zing to this mix of beets and spinach, adding even more vitamin C and antioxidants to an already healthful mix. Garnet-fleshed blood oranges, at their peak of flavor in winter, can be used in place of the navel oranges. Add some protein with a sprinkling of toasted walnuts or almonds if you like.

Beets, 4 small (about ½ lb/225 g total weight), trimmed

Lemon juice, 1 tablespoon, plus more to taste

Shallot, 1, minced

Sea salt and freshly ground pepper

Extra-virgin olive oil, 3 tablespoons

Navel oranges, 2 large

Baby spinach, 6 cups (6 oz/170 g)

MAKES 6 SERVINGS

1. Preheat the oven to 375°F (190°C).

2. Wrap the beets in foil, place on a rimmed baking sheet, and roast until easily pierced with a paring knife, 45–60 minutes. Remove from the oven and let cool in the foil.

3. Meanwhile, to make the dressing, in a small bowl, combine the lemon juice and shallot. Season to taste with salt and pepper. Let stand for 30 minutes to allow the shallot flavor to mellow, then add the oil in a thin stream, whisking constantly until the dressing is well blended.

4. Cut a slice off the top and bottom of each orange. Stand each upright and, following the contour of the fruit, cut away all the peel and white pith. Cut along both sides of each segment to free it from the membrane.

5. When the beets are cool enough to handle, peel and cut them into wedges about the size of the orange segments. Place the beet wedges in a bowl and toss with just enough of the dressing to coat them lightly.

6. Place the spinach in a large bowl and add the orange segments. Add the remaining dressing and toss to coat. Season to taste with salt, pepper, and more lemon juice.

7. Divide the spinach and oranges among plates. Arrange the beets on top and serve right away.

FRESH VEGETABLE SPRING ROLLS

These satisfying, nutritional spring rolls are packed with fresh herbs and vegetables and make a healthy side dish, starter, or light meal; serve them with prepared chile and peanut dipping sauces. The carrots are an excellent source of vitamin A while the shiitake mushrooms provide B vitamins and potassium and can help boost immunity. Change up the filling ingredients with other veggies as you please.

Shiitake mushrooms, ½ lb (250 g)

Canola or peanut oil, 2 teaspoons

Garlic, 1 clove, pressed or minced

Soy sauce, 1 teaspoon

Thin dried rice noodles, 7 oz (220 g)

Rice-paper wrappers, 12
(8½ inches/21.5 cm in diameter)

Red bell pepper, 1, seeded and thinly sliced

Ripe avocados, 2, pitted, peeled, and sliced

Carrots, 2, peeled and cut into matchsticks

Mixed fresh herb sprigs such as mint, cilantro, and basil, 1 cup packed (1 oz/30 g)

MAKES 6-8 SERVINGS

1. Trim stems from the shiitakes and discard (or save for soup or stock). Slice caps and set aside. In a large nonstick frying pan, heat 1 teaspoon oil over medium-high heat. Add the garlic and cook, stirring, until fragrant but not browned, about 30 seconds. Add the mushrooms and sauté until they have released their juices, 3–4 minutes. Add the soy sauce and cook until the pan is dry, about 1 minute. Transfer to a bowl and set aside.

2. Bring a pot of water to a boil over high heat. Add the noodles, stir to separate, and cook until tender, 3–5 minutes or according to package directions. Drain in a colander and rinse under cold running water. Wipe the pot dry, return the noodles to pot, and toss with the remaining 1 teaspoon oil.

3. Fill a large, shallow bowl with very hot tap water. Soak the rice-paper wrappers, 1 or 2 at a time, until flexible, about 30 seconds. Shake off any excess water and stack on a plate. Place 1 wrapper flat on a work surface. Arrange a combination of noodles, bell pepper, avocado, mushrooms, carrots, and herbs across the center of the wrapper; fold the ends in over the filling, then roll up tightly from the edge closest to you. Repeat to make more rolls.

4. Cut the rolls in half on diagonal and serve right away.

THE WHYS OF BUYING LOCAL & ORGANIC

In an era when much of our food supply is falling into the hands of a few multinational corporations,[1] the solution is surprisingly simple: we must turn our attention—and our dollars—back to our local economies and focus on sustainability.

By purchasing from local producers and suppliers, we support the valued members of our community: those who grow, those who produce, those who distribute, and those who sell. And the wealth comes back to us in the form of a more stable and thriving economy.[2]

When we purchase locally grown products that are also organic, we are helping to protect the environment. To be USDA-certified organic, rigorous standards must be met. For produce, this means harmful chemicals like pesticides stay out of our soil, the surrounding environment is not destroyed, and genetically modified seeds are not being planted.[3]

"The real cost of industrial farming never shows up on the price sticker at the grocery store... The grocery store price also doesn't reflect how much we pay for our damaged health and weakened immune systems. It's almost impossible to measure how much we spend trying to clean up and cope with the environmental damage caused by chemical-intensive farming." [4]

---

[1] Oxfam, Hoffman, B. 2014. Behind the Brands. https://www.oxfam.org/en/research/behind-brands.

[2] Ward, Bernie, Julie Lewis, New Economics Foundation, Esmée Fairbairn Foundation, and Great Britain. Neighbourhood Renewal Unit. 2002. *Plugging the Leaks: Making the Most of Every Pound That Enters Your Local Economy*. London: New Economics Foundation.

[3] "Organic Regulations | Agricultural Marketing Service." Usda.Gov. United States Departent of Agriculture. 2019. https://www.ams.usda.gov/rules-regulations/organic.

[4] Goodall, McAvoy, and Hudson, *Harvest for Hope*, 169.

All of this can be balanced—remembering that finding affordable food that is plant-based is just as important as seeking out organic and local foods. It's important to remember that *every choice is a balance, and even if you check all these boxes, there are always new ways to think about the impact of your food.* For example, although almond milk is a great replacement for cow's milk, producing and processing the almonds can be water-intensive.[6] Though it may use fewer resources than industrial agriculture, it may still be worth exploring other options depending on availability. Other examples are avocado, olive and palm oils. These powerhouse plant-based oils are incredibly good for us and better options, but industrialized versions of these products can be water-intensive, degrade soil, and heavily rely on chemicals and monocultures. As a solution, check the labels and consider only responsibly derived plant-based oils. Thinking about your daily choices and buying local and organic plant-based products ensures that our dollars stay in our own economies, fights climate change by reducing transportation, protects our environment at home, and provides our community members with the opportunity they need to thrive—making it a simple and effective solution for changing our food system.

---

[6] Fleischer, Deborah. 2018. "Almond Milk is Taking a Toll on the Environment." UCSF.edu. University of California San Francisco. 2018. https://sustainability.ucsf.edu/1.713.

MAINS

"An easy way to get started is to eat one local, seasonal meal a week. Make a social occasion of it, invite family and friends to help, organize a seasonal foods potluck where recipes and resources are exchanged."—Jane

LEMONGRASS TOFU BÁNH MÌ

In this flavorful version of the Vietnamese baguette sandwich, marinated tofu is a satisfying, protein-rich centerpiece. Add tangy pickled vegetables and a quick, spicy mayonnaise and you'll be hooked. Look for organic, sustainable tofu, which is better for the environment and provides clean, inexpensive protein.

Fresh lemongrass (white bulb part only), 1 tablespoon finely chopped

Garlic, 1 tablespoon finely chopped

Sriracha, 2 teaspoons

Lime juice, 2 teaspoons

Organic sugar, 2 teaspoons

Sea salt and freshly ground pepper

Canola oil, ¼ cup (2 fl oz/60 ml) plus 2 tablespoons

Extra-firm tofu, 1 lb (450 g), patted dry and cut into 12 slabs ¼ inch (6 mm) thick

Vegan mayonnaise, ½ cup (4 fl oz/120 ml)

Daikon, ¾ cup (4 oz/115 g) grated

Carrot, ¾ cup (4 oz/115 g) grated

Rice vinegar, 1 tablespoon

Vietnamese-style baguette rolls or hoagie buns, 4

Fresh cilantro leaves, 1 cup (1 oz/30 g)

Jalapeño chile, 1 large, thinly sliced

MAKES 4 SERVINGS

1. In a mini food processor or using a mortar and pestle, pulse or pound the lemongrass, garlic, Sriracha, lime juice, 1 teaspoon of the sugar, and ½ teaspoon each salt and pepper until a paste forms. Add 2 tablespoons of the oil and blend well. Coat the tofu pieces using 3 tablespoons of the lemongrass paste; set aside. Stir together the remaining paste and the vegan mayonnaise and set aside.

2. In a small bowl, stir together the daikon, carrot, vinegar, remaining 1 teaspoon sugar, and ½ teaspoon salt; set aside.

3. In a large nonstick frying pan, warm the remaining ¼ cup (2 fl oz/60 ml) oil over medium-high heat. Add the tofu and fry until golden brown and crisp, about 2 minutes per side. Transfer to a paper towel–lined plate.

4. Cut open the rolls horizontally, leaving one long side of the bun partially attached. Spread the lemongrass mayonnaise evenly on the inside of the rolls. Place 3 tofu slabs on each bun and top with the daikon-carrot salad, cilantro, and jalapeño. Serve right away.

Recipe note

To make the thin vegetable cuts for this recipe, consider investing in a julienne peeler, a handy rakelike device that makes perfect julienne strips out of firm vegetables like daikon and carrot. Look for the tool at kitchenware stores and online. Because lemongrass is a tough stem to chop, buy packaged minced lemongrass.

QUINOA, CRISPY CHICKPEA & SEASONAL VEGGIE BOWL WITH SESAME-TURMERIC SAUCE

Quinoa is often described as the grain with "complete protein" because it contains all nine essential amino acids. Beyond the protein, quinoa is a nutritional powerhouse, bringing respectable amounts of fiber, calcium, and minerals to the plate in a delicious, nutty tasting package. In this bowl, you can riff with whatever vegetables are in season, and top it off with a turmeric-laced sauce made from creamy tahini.

FOR THE SESAME-TURMERIC SAUCE

Tahini, ¼ cup (2½ oz/70 g)

Maple syrup, 1 tablespoon

Ground turmeric, ¼ teaspoon

Garlic, 1 clove, pressed

Apple cider vinegar, 1 tablespoon

Soy sauce, 1 tablespoon

Quinoa, 1½ cups (12 oz/340 g)

Chickpeas, 1 can (15 oz/425 g), drained, rinsed, and patted dry

Extra-virgin olive oil, 1 tablespoon

Smoked paprika, 1 teaspoon

Ground cumin, ½ teaspoon

Sea salt

Carrot, 1 large, shredded

Grape tomatoes, 1 cup (6 oz/170 g), halved

Cauliflower florets, 2 cups (4 oz/115 g)

Sauerkraut or kimchi, ½ cup (2½ oz/70 g) drained and chopped (optional)

Avocado, 1 large, pitted, peeled, and sliced

1. In a saucepan, bring 2¼ cups (18 fl oz/525 ml) water to a boil. Add the quinoa and return to a boil. Cover, reduce the heat to low, and cook until the water is absorbed, about 15 minutes. Remove from the heat and let stand, covered, until serving.

2. To make the sesame-turmeric sauce, in a small bowl, use a fork to stir together the tahini, maple syrup, turmeric, and garlic until smooth. Add the vinegar, soy sauce, and 2 tablespoons water and stir until well combined. (You can also just combine the ingredients in a blender and process until smooth.)

3. Preheat the oven to 400°F (200°C).

   Place the chickpeas on a on a rimmed baking sheet, drizzle with the oil, and toss to coat. Roast, shaking the pan halfway through, until the chickpeas are browned, about 25 minutes. Remove from the oven and sprinkle with the paprika, cumin, and ½ teaspoon salt.

4. Place one-fourth of the cooked quinoa in each of 4 wide bowls. Arrange the carrot, tomatoes, cauliflower, sauerkraut (if using), avocado, and crispy chickpeas on top. Drizzle with the sauce and serve right away.

MAKES 4 SERVINGS

INDONESIAN-STYLE VEGETABLE SALAD WITH TEMPEH

This crisp and crunchy salad with a curry-cashew dip gets a protein boost from the fermented soybeans in tempeh. The dense, chewy cake is a food originating in Indonesia, where it has long been a central part of many recipes. Feel free to play with the vegetables and fruits according to the season and your whim.

Jasmine rice, 1 cup (7 oz/200 g)

Ground turmeric, ½ teaspoon

Sea salt

Hot water, ¼ cup (2 fl oz/60 ml)

Roasted salted cashews, ½ cup (2½ oz/70 g)

Lime juice, ¼ cup (2 fl oz/60 ml)

Soy sauce, 1 tablespoon

Vegan Thai red curry paste, 1 tablespoon

Brown sugar, 1 tablespoon

Broccoli florets, 2 cups (4 oz/115 g)

Green beans, 6 oz (170 g), cut into 2-inch (5-cm) pieces

English cucumber, 1, peeled, halved lengthwise, and cut crosswise into ¼-inch (6-mm) slices

Fresh pineapple, 6 oz (170 g), cut into chunks

Red bell pepper, ½, seeded and thinly sliced

Canola oil, 1½ tablespoons

Marinated tempeh strips (such as Tofurky coconut curry flavor), ½ lb (225 g)

1. In a small saucepan, combine the rice, turmeric, ½ teaspoon salt, and 2 cups (16 fl oz/475 ml) water. Bring to a boil, reduce the heat to low, cover, and simmer until tender, 12–15 minutes.

2. In a food processor, combine the hot water, cashews, lime juice, soy sauce, curry paste, and brown sugar and process until smooth. Pour the mixture into a small serving bowl and set aside.

3. Bring a saucepan of water to a boil. Fill a bowl with ice water. Add the broccoli to the boiling water and cook for about 2 minutes. Add the green beans and cook until tender-crisp, about 2 minutes. Drain the vegetables and plunge them into the ice water to stop them from cooking. When cool, drain and pat dry with paper towels. On a large platter, arrange the broccoli, green beans, cucumber, pineapple, and bell pepper.

4. In a large nonstick frying pan, warm the oil over medium-high heat. Add the tempeh strips and cook until golden brown and crisp, about 2 minutes per side. Drain on paper towels and add to the platter. Serve right away, with the cashew sauce and rice on the side.

MAKES 4 SERVINGS

Recipe note

You can skip the chopping and the blanching in step 2 by visiting the salad bar at your local market and filling a to-go container with your favorite vegetables. Bring them home and arrange on a platter with the tempeh.

SOBA NOODLES WITH ASPARAGUS & MUSHROOMS

This Japanese-inspired noodle dish highlights asparagus at its peak in early spring. Wakame, a sustainable, mineral-rich sea vegetable, adds a briny counterpoint to the slippery noodles and crisp asparagus spears. Shiitake mushrooms are famous for their umami-rich, meaty qualities, as well as potent levels of healthful chemicals.

Dried wakame or mixed sea vegetables, 2 tablespoons

Soy sauce, 2 tablespoons

Rice vinegar, 2 tablespoons

Organic sugar, 1 tablespoon

Toasted sesame oil, 2 teaspoons

Soba noodles, ½ lb (225 g)

Canola oil, 2 tablespoons

Fresh ginger, 2 teaspoons peeled and finely grated

Garlic, 2 teaspoons finely chopped

Asparagus, ¾ lb (340 g), tough ends snapped off and spears cut into 2-inch (5-cm) pieces

Shiitake mushrooms, 3 oz (90 g), stems discarded and caps sliced

MAKES 4 SERVINGS

1. In a small bowl, combine the wakame and 1 cup (8 fl oz/250 ml) water. Set aside to reconstitute for 15 minutes. Drain the wakame, squeeze out the excess water, and set aside.

2. In another small bowl, whisk together the soy sauce, vinegar, sugar, and sesame oil until the sugar dissolves; set aside.

3. Bring a pot of water to a boil. Add the soba noodles and cook until just tender, about 4 minutes. Drain and rinse with cool water to stop them from cooking; set aside.

4. In a wok or large nonstick frying pan, warm the canola oil over medium-high heat. Add the ginger and garlic and stir-fry until aromatic, 20 seconds. Add the asparagus and mushrooms and stir-fry for about 1 minute. Add 2 tablespoons water, cover, and cook until the asparagus is tender-crisp and bright green, about 2 minutes, depending on its thickness.

5. Uncover, remove the pan from the heat, and add the noodles and soy sauce mixture, tossing to coat. Divide the noodle-vegetable mixture among shallow bowls. Top the noodles with the wakame and serve warm or chilled.

Recipe note

If you're crunched for time, you can substitute fresh yakisoba (available in the produce department of most grocery stores) for the soba: just drop the pre-cooked noodles directly into the wok in Step 5 above to reheat them.

GRILLED EGGPLANT BRUSCHETTA WITH HAZELNUT SKORDALIA

Look for shiny purple baby eggplants for this summery bruschetta. Tangy skordalia—as delectable as cheese but without the dairy—brightens the earthy flavor and showcases hazelnuts, a sustainable crop harvested from trees that thrive in poor soils with little water.

8 baby eggplants (about 1 lb/ 450 g total), sliced lengthwise

Olive oil, ¼ cup (2 fl oz/60 ml)

Sea salt

Balsamic vinegar, 1½ tablespoons

Maple syrup, 1 tablespoon

Sourdough bread, 1 loaf

FOR THE HAZELNUT SKORDALIA

Skinless hazelnuts, ¾ cup (3½ oz/100 g)

Garlic, 2 large cloves, crushed

Lemon juice, 1½ tablespoons

Red wine vinegar, 2 teaspoons

Olive oil, ¼ cup (2 fl oz/60 ml)

1 leaf red lettuce or raddichio, shredded

Lemon zest, finely grated, 2 teaspoons

MAKES 4 SERVINGS

1. Brush the eggplant slices on both sides with 2 tablespoons of the oil and season with salt. Heat a grill pan over medium-high heat. Add the eggplant and cook until just tender, about 3 minutes per side. (Alternatively, cook on a rimmed baking sheet under a preheated broiler.) Transfer to a medium bowl, add the vinegar and maple syrup, and toss to coat.

2. Cut the rounded ends off the bread and reserve for the skordalia. Cut the remaining bread into 8 thick slices and brush on both sides with the remaining 2 tablespoons oil. Toast the bread on a heated grill pan until grill marks appear, about 2 minutes per side. (Alternatively, toast the bread under a broiler.)

3. To make the skordalia, preheat the oven to 350°F (180°C). Spread out the hazelnuts on a rimmed baking sheet. Roast until golden brown, about 8 minutes; let cool. Chop one-third of the nuts and reserve for serving. Transfer the remaining nuts to a food processor and process until finely ground. Add the reserved bread and process until finely crumbled. Add the garlic, lemon juice, vinegar, oil, and ¾ cup (6 fl oz/180 ml) water and process until combined. Season to taste with salt.

4. Spread each sourdough toast generously with the skordalia. Top with the eggplant slices, some lettuce, reserved hazelnuts, and lemon zest. Serve right away.

Recipe notes

You can use zucchini instead of eggplant, and almonds or walnuts instead of hazelnuts, if you like. For bite-size bruschetta, use a sliced sourdough baguette for the toasts and cut the eggplant into smaller pieces.

Skordalia can be made up to 1 week ahead; keep in a covered container in the fridge.

EDAMAME & AVOCADO QUESADILLAS WITH RASPBERRY SALSA

Quesadillas are a quick weeknight meal usually filled with cheese. This version of the crispy triangles, made with a creamy avocado-edamame purée, delivers all the same satisfaction without the dairy. Instead of pairing them with jarred salsa, make an easy raspberry-mint salsa for a summertime surprise. Edamame is a protein-rich green soybean, available frozen and already hulled, for a convenient, unprocessed meat alternative.

FOR THE RASPBERRY SALSA

Raspberries, 2 cups (8 oz/225 g)

Fresno or jalapeño chile, 1 large red, seeded and minced

Fresh mint, ½ cup (¾ oz/20 g) chopped

Green onion, ¼ cup (¾ oz/20 g) finely chopped

Organic sugar, 1 teaspoon

Sea salt

Frozen shelled edamame, 1 cup (6 oz/170 g), thawed

Garlic, 2 cloves

Fresh cilantro, ½ cup (¾ oz/20 g) chopped

Ripe avocado, 1 large, pitted and peeled

Whole-wheat tortillas (9 inches/23 cm), 4

MAKES 2 SERVINGS

1. To make the salsa, place the raspberries in a medium bowl. Add the chile, mint, green onion, sugar, and ½ teaspoon salt and toss gently to mix. Set aside.

2. In a food processor, combine the edamame, garlic, and cilantro and process until smooth. Add the avocado and ¾ teaspoon salt and purée until well mixed.

3. Scrape the edamame mixture into a medium bowl. Place 2 tortillas on a cutting board and spread about half of the purée on each one. Place the remaining 2 tortillas on top of the filling and press lightly to adhere.

4. Heat a large frying pan over medium-high heat until very hot, about 2 minutes. Carefully place a quesadilla in the pan and cook for 1 minute, then use a spatula to peek underneath. When the tortilla is spotted with brown, flip the quesadilla and cook until spotted with brown, about 1 minute more.

5. Slide the quesadilla onto the cutting board and use a chef's knife or pizza wheel to cut into 6 wedges. Repeat with the remaining quesadilla. Serve the quesadillas right away with the salsa.

SEITAN & VEGETABLE STIR-FRY WITH BLACK BEAN SAUCE

You can throw together this colorful plant-based stir-fry in minutes. Chewy seitan, made from cooked wheat gluten, takes the place of meat, and umami-rich black bean–garlic sauce helps make a quick, deeply flavorful seasoning sauce. Bok choy is a wonderfully crunchy, authentic presence in this dish, but if you can't find any, sub in a few stalks of baby broccoli.

Black bean–garlic sauce, 3 tablespoons

Chinese rice wine or dry sherry, 2 tablespoons

Soy sauce, 1 tablespoon

Cornstarch, 2 teaspoons

Canola oil, 2 tablespoons

Seitan, ½ lb (225 g), drained and thinly sliced

Fresh ginger, 1 tablespoon peeled and finely chopped

Baby bok choy, 2 large heads, white stems cut into 1-inch (2.5-cm) slices, greens left whole

Red bell pepper, 1 small, seeded and sliced

Shiitake mushrooms, 4 oz (115 g), stems discarded and caps sliced

Steamed rice, for serving

MAKES 4 SERVINGS

1. In a small bowl, whisk together the black bean–garlic sauce, rice wine, soy sauce, cornstarch, and 2 tablespoons water; set aside.

2. In a wok or large frying pan, warm 1 tablespoon of the oil over high heat. When the oil is nearly smoking, add the seitan and stir-fry until lightly seared around the edges, about 1 minute. Transfer to a bowl and set aside. Reduce the heat to medium-high and add the remaining 1 tablespoon oil. Add the ginger and stir-fry until aromatic, about 10 seconds. Add the bok choy, bell pepper, and mushrooms and stir-fry until the vegetables are tender-crisp, about 2 minutes.

3. Return the seitan to the wok. Stir in the black bean–garlic sauce mixture and stir-fry until the sauce is thick and bubbly, about 1 minute. Serve right away with the rice.

Recipe note

Black bean–garlic sauce is an ideal condiment for plant-based cooking because even just a small amount of fermented black beans adds a big punch of umami. Thin the sauce with vinegar and oil to make a dressing for steamed vegetables or egg noodles, or a marinade for tofu. An opened jar of black bean–garlic sauce will last for months in the refrigerator.

CHICKPEA, SPINACH & CARROT CURRY

This warm, comforting stew is seasoned with *panch phoron*, a Bengali five-spice blend. It's a combination of one part each of cumin seed, black mustard seed, nigella seed, fennel seed, and one-half part fenugreek seed—make the blend yourself if you can't find it in stores or online. Serve the curry with whole-grain naan or steamed basmati rice and chutney on the side.

Canola oil, 2 tablespoons

Panch phoron, 2 teaspoons

Yellow onion, ½, thinly sliced

Carrots, 2 large, peeled and thinly sliced on the bias

Fresh ginger, 2 tablespoons peeled and finely chopped

Garlic, 1 tablespoon finely chopped

Canned chopped tomatoes, 3 cups (26½ oz/750 g)

Chickpeas, 1 can (15 oz/425 g), drained and rinsed

Baby spinach, 2 cups (2 oz/60 g) loosely packed

Sea salt and freshly ground pepper

MAKES 4 SERVINGS

1. In a large sauté pan, warm the oil over medium heat. Add the panch phoron and and cook, stirring, until fragrant, about 1 minute. Add the onion and carrots and cook, stirring, until they start to brown, about 5 minutes. Add the ginger and garlic and cook, stirring occasionally, until fragrant, about 1 minute.

2. Add the tomatoes and chickpeas and bring to a simmer. Cook, stirring occasionally, until the carrots are tender and the sauce has thickened a bit, about 15 minutes. Add the spinach and simmer until wilted, about 5 minutes. Season to taste with salt and pepper. Divide among bowls and serve right away.

Recipe note

Legumes release less greenhouse-gas emissions than other crops, giving them a sustainability edge. Also, they can make their own nitrogen from the atmosphere, reducing the need to apply nitrogen fertilizers to legume crops. Chickpeas, part of the legume family, are high in protein and low in fat, making them an excellent substitute for meat. They're also packed with nutrients, including iron, phosphate, calcium, zinc, and magnesium. A staple of diets all over the world (chickpeas are grown on every continent except for Antarctica), chickpeas are endlessly versatile—they blend well with a broad range of ingredients and seasonings and can be cooked countless ways.

SESAME NOODLES WITH GREEN BEANS & TOFU

Sesame noodle dishes are classic, and adding some baked tofu makes them into a complete meal. Once you make baked tofu, you'll want to keep it in your rotation. It's a great item to have on hand as a savory, chewy protein to use in soups, stir-fries, sandwiches, and noodle dishes all week long.

Extra-firm tofu, 12 oz (340 g)

Tamari, 2 tablespoons plus ¼ cup (2 fl oz/60 ml)

Toasted sesame oil, 1 tablespoon

Tahini, 3 tablespoons

Rice vinegar, 1 tablespoon

Hot sesame oil, 1 tablespoon

Fresh ginger, 1 tablespoon peeled and minced

Garlic, 4 cloves, pressed

Organic sugar, 1 teaspoon

Whole-wheat spaghetti, 1 lb (450 g)

Green beans, 2 cups (4 oz/115 g), trimmed and cut into 2-inch (5-cm) pieces

English cucumber, 1, peeled and sliced

Green onions, 4, thinly sliced

Peanuts, roasted and unsalted, ¼ cup (1¼ oz/35 g) chopped

MAKES 6 SERVINGS

1. Preheat the oven to 400°F (200°C).

2. To press the tofu, drain, wrap in a thick kitchen towel, and place on a plate. Place a heavy pan or cutting board on top and let stand for about 5 minutes. Unwrap and pat dry with another towel. Transfer to a cutting board and cut into cubes.

3. Place the tofu on a rimmed baking sheet and drizzle with 2 tablespoons of the tamari and the toasted sesame oil. Toss carefully to coat. Roast for 20 minutes, then flip with a metal offset spatula and roast until lightly browned, about 10 minutes more. Remove from the oven and keep warm.

4. In a large bowl, whisk together the remaining ¼ cup (2 fl oz/60 ml) tamari, the tahini, vinegar, hot sesame oil, ginger, garlic, and sugar until smooth.

5. Bring a pot of water to a boil. Add the spaghetti to the boiling water and cook according to package instructions, adding the green beans for the last 2 minutes. Drain.

6. Add the spaghetti, beans, and tofu to the tahini mixture and toss to coat. Spread on a platter and top with the cucumber, green onions, and peanuts. Serve right away.

BLACK BEAN–AVOCADO SOPES

In Mexico, small fried masa cakes are often filled with shredded meat. Here, they're topped with a plant-based medley of refried black beans, salsa, and avocado. Though they are vegan and petite, they're actually quite filling—three sopes make a meal. Once you buy a bag of masa, you'll want to prepare these all the time and enjoy the delicious corn flavor.

Masa Dough for Sopes (page 160)

Extra-virgin olive oil, 1 tablespoon

Yellow onion, 1 large, finely chopped (7 oz/200 g)

Cumin seeds, 1½ teaspoons

Black beans, 2 cans (15 oz/425 g each), drained and rinsed

Tomatoes, 2 cups (12 oz/340 g) diced

Fresh cilantro, ½ cup (¾ oz/20 g) chopped

Jalapeño chile, 1, finely chopped

Lime juice, 1 tablespoon

Sea salt

Canola oil, 1½ cups (12 fl oz/350 ml)

Romaine lettuce, 2 cups (2 oz/60 g) finely shredded

Ripe avocados, 2 small, pitted, peeled, and sliced or cut into cubes

MAKES 4 SERVINGS

1. Preheat the oven to 200°F (95°C). Meanwhile, make the dough for the sope shells.

2. In a saucepan, warm the olive oil over medium-high heat. Add 1 cup (5 oz/140 g) of the onion and the cumin seeds and cook, stirring occasionally, until the onion starts to brown, about 2 minutes. Add the beans and mash with a potato masher until nearly smooth. Add 1 cup (8 fl oz/240 ml) water and bring to a simmer. Reduce the heat to low and keep warm. In a bowl, stir together the remaining ⅓ cup (2 oz/60 g) onion, the tomatoes, cilantro, jalapeño, and lime juice. Season the beans and the salsa to taste with salt.

3. In a deep cast-iron pan, warm the canola oil over medium-high heat until it reaches 350°F (180°C) on a deep-frying thermometer. Meanwhile, press the masa balls between your palms and then transfer them to a sheet of parchment paper. Pat them out with your fingertips until they are about 3 inches (7.5 cm) in diameter. Pinch up the edges to form little tart shells. Cover the completed shells with parchment paper as you work.

4. When the oil is ready, fry the shells in batches of 3 until golden brown and crisp, 2–3 minutes. Transfer the fried shells to a baking sheet and keep them warm in the oven while frying the remaining ones.

5. Divide the bean mixture among the fried masa shells. Top evenly with the salsa, lettuce, and avocado. Serve right away.

PAN-FRIED FALAFEL WITH CUMIN & GARLIC

Keeping some dried chickpeas in the pantry guarantees that you have a sustainable, high-protein food at your fingertips, ready to make these crunchy falafel. Soaked and barely cooked chickpeas are the key to their pleasing texture. Tuck the savory Middle Eastern patties into warmed pita bread rounds along with a lettuce leaf, a spoonful of chopped tomatoes, a dollop of tahini, and a sprinkling of fresh mint. Keep the cooked falafel warm in a low (200°F/95°C) oven while you finish pan-frying the rest.

Dried chickpeas, 1½ cups (10½ oz/300 g)

Yellow onion, 1, chopped

Garlic, 3 cloves, chopped

Fresh flat-leaf parsley leaves, 1 cup (1 oz/30 g) packed

Baking powder, 1 teaspoon

Ground cumin, 1 teaspoon

Sea salt

Red pepper flakes, ½ teaspoon

Olive oil, 1 tablespoon plus more as needed

Pita bread, lettuce, chopped tomatoes, tahini, and mint, for serving

MAKES 4 SERVINGS

1. Bring a large pot of lightly salted water to a boil. Add the chickpeas and cook until slightly softened but still very firm in the center, about 10 minutes. Drain and cool slightly

2. In a food processor, combine the chickpeas, onion, garlic, and parsley and process until coarsely puréed. Transfer the mixture to a bowl and stir in the baking powder, cumin, ¾ teaspoon salt, and red pepper flakes. Refrigerate the mixture until cold, about 1 hour.

3. In a large nonstick frying pan, warm the oil over medium-high heat. With dampened hands, shape ¼-cup (60-g) portions of the chickpea mixture into patties about 3 inches (7.5 cm) in diameter. Place 3 or 4 patties at a time in the pan and cook, turning once, until browned on both sides, 4–6 minutes total. Repeat to shape and cook the remaining falafel, adding more oil to the pan as needed.

4. Tuck 1 falafel into each pita bread and serve with the lettuce, tomatoes, tahini, and mint.

BROCCOLI-KALE CHICKPEA FRITTATA

If an eggy frittata was your go-to easy dinner recipe in the past, try this chickpea flour version instead. Also known as besan, chickpea flour is a traditional ingredient in Indian cooking. Now that it is widely used in gluten-free and vegan recipes, it's usually available locally. Sustainable, healthy chickpeas are transformed into a tasty stand-in for eggs just by mixing the flour with water. Kala nemak, or Himalayan black salt, is a roasted sulfurous seasoning from South Asia that gives foods an eggy flavor.

Extra-virgin olive oil, 1 tablespoon

Yellow onion, 1 cup (4 oz/115 g) chopped

Broccoli, 2 cups (8 oz/225 g) chopped

Kale, stems removed, 2 cups (4 oz/115 g) chopped leaves

Sea salt

Chickpea flour, 1½ cups (4½ oz/130 g)

Tomato paste, 1 tablespoon

Kala nemak or other salt replacement, 1 teaspoon

Ground turmeric, ½ teaspoon

Freshly ground pepper

MAKES 6 SERVINGS

1. Preheat the oven to 375°F (190°C). Use 1 teaspoon of the oil to grease a deep-dish pie pan.

2. Place a large dry sauté pan over medium-high heat and add the remaining oil, onion, and broccoli. Cook, stirring and reducing the heat to medium when the vegetables start to sizzle, until they are tender, about 4 minutes. Remove from the heat and stir in the kale and ½ teaspoon salt. Let stand until the kale wilts.

3. In a medium bowl, whisk together the chickpea flour and 1½ cups (12 fl oz/350 ml) water until smooth. Add the tomato paste, kala nemak, turmeric, and ½ teaspoon pepper. Stir the cooked vegetables into the chickpea mixture, then scrape into the prepared pie pan.

4. Bake until the top is cracked and feels firm when pressed, about 45 minutes. Cool in the pan on a rack for 5 minutes before slicing into 6 wedges. Serve right away. The frittata can be stored, tightly covered in the refrigerator, for up to 4 days.

CREAMY CASHEW PASTA PRIMAVERA

If you're craving creamy pasta, this cashew-based sauce will more than satisfy. Use the unsweetened nondairy milk of your choice, and build in some umami and cheesy flavor with miso and nutritional yeast. Whole-wheat pasta is a most healthful pairing with this sauce, and because the bran and germ in whole grains slow digestion, you will stay full longer.

Raw cashews, 1 cup (5 oz/140 g), soaked overnight

Vegetable broth, ½ cup (4 fl oz/ 120 ml), plus more as needed

Unsweetened nondairy milk, ½ cup (4 fl oz/120 ml)

White miso, 1 tablespoon

Nutritional yeast, 1 tablespoon (optional)

Extra-virgin olive oil, 1 tablespoon

Yellow onion, 1 large, chopped

Garlic, 2 cloves, chopped

Vegan white wine, ½ cup (4 fl oz/120 ml)

Sea salt and freshly ground pepper

Whole-wheat fettuccine, ½ lb (225 g)

Asparagus, 1 lb (450 g), tough ends snapped off, spears cut into 2-inch (5-cm) pieces

Carrots, 2 large (5 oz/140 g total), peeled and diced or julienned

Cauliflower florets, 2 cups (4 oz/115 g)

Frozen peas, ½ cup (2½ oz/90 g)

Grape tomatoes, ½ cup (3 oz/85 g) halved

Fresh flat-leaf parsley, ¼ cup (⅓ oz/10 g) chopped

1. Drain the cashews well, then place them in a blender or food processor. Blend to a paste. Add the broth, nondairy milk, miso, and nutritional yeast (if using) and blend until smooth. Set aside.

2. In a large sauté pan, warm the oil over medium heat. Add the onion and cook, stirring occasionally and reducing the heat to prevent browning, until the onion is golden and very soft, about 30 minutes. Add the garlic and cook, stirring occasionally, until fragrant, about 5 minutes. Scrape the onion mixture into the blender with the cashew mixture. Add the wine and process until very smooth. Season to taste with salt and pepper.

3. Bring a large pot of salted water to a boil. Add the fettuccine and cook according to package instructions, adding the asparagus, carrots, cauliflower, peas, and tomatoes for the last 2 minutes. Drain well.

4. Transfer the contents of the blender to the empty pasta pot and heat, stirring, over medium heat. Add the hot pasta and vegetables to the pot. Stir and toss and if it seems thin, cook for a few minutes longer to thicken the sauce; if the sauce seems too thick, stir in a little broth or water 1 tablespoon at a time until the desired consistency is reached. Sprinkle with the parsley and serve right away.

MAKES 4–6 SERVINGS

LEFTOVER-GRAIN FRIED RICE WITH SEITAN & PEANUTS

A classic way to recycle leftovers, fried rice is so beloved it has made it onto the menus of restaurants the world over. By tossing a cooked grain of any type into a hot pan with vegetables, a protein, and seasonings, you can create a crave-worthy meal. Use whole grains for more fiber and minerals, and prepare extra so you can throw together a satisfying dish like this the next day.

Cooked grain (such as brown rice or quinoa), 1 cup (5 oz/155 g), chilled

Fresh ginger, 1 tablespoon peeled and chopped

Garlic, 2 cloves, chopped

Soy sauce, 2 tablespoons

Tahini, 2 tablespoons

Rice vinegar, 2 tablespoons

Toasted sesame oil, 1 teaspoon

Avocado oil, 1 tablespoon

Yellow onion, 1 small, chopped

Broccoli florets, 2 cups (4 oz/115 g)

Red bell pepper, ½ large, seeded and sliced

Seitan or mock duck, 10 oz (285 g), cut into bite-size pieces

Green onions, 4, cut into 1-inch (2.5-cm) pieces

Roasted unsalted peanuts, ½ cup (3 oz/90 g) coarsely chopped

MAKES 4 SERVINGS

1. Let the grain come to room temperature and break up any lumps with your fingers. In a small bowl, stir together the ginger, garlic, soy sauce, tahini, vinegar, and sesame oil and set aside.

2. In a wok or large frying pan, warm the avocado oil over medium-high heat until hot, swirling to coat the pan. Add the onion, broccoli, and bell pepper and and stir-fry until the vegetables are tender-crisp, about 2 minutes. Add the seitan and stir until heated through and starting to brown, about 2 minutes. Add the grain and drizzle the tahini mixture over it. Stir and turn the contents of the pan until the grain is heated through and the mixture looks dry, about 2 minutes. Stir in the green onions and serve right away, sprinkled with the peanuts.

BAKED BARLEY & LENTIL PILAF WITH EGGPLANT

In this baked pilaf, the oven's heat gently brings the eggplant to tender perfection as it simmers with the barley and lentils. Look for black, beluga, or French lentils for this dish, as these are all small round lentils that hold their shape when cooked. Both barley and lentils are heart-healthy, cholesterol-lowering foods.

Extra-virgin olive oil, 2 tablespoons

Yellow onion, 1 large, chopped

Garlic, 2 cloves, chopped

Globe eggplant, 1, 11 oz (310 g), peeled and chopped

Roma tomato, 1 large, chopped

Dried thyme, 1 teaspoon

Dried oregano, 1 teaspoon

Ground turmeric, ½ teaspoon

Pearled barley, 1 cup (7 oz/200 g), rinsed and drained

Dried black lentils, 1 cup (7 oz/200 g), rinsed and drained

Vegan white wine, ½ cup (4 fl oz/120 ml)

Sea salt

Fresh flat-leaf parsley, ½ cup (¾ oz/20 g) chopped

MAKES 6 SERVINGS

1. Preheat the oven to 350°F (180°C).

2. In an oven-safe 3-quart (3-l) baking dish, warm the oil over medium-high heat. Add the onion and cook, stirring occasionally and reducing the heat to medium-low when they start to sizzle, until starting to soften, about 5 minutes. Add the garlic and cook, stirring, until fragrant, about 1 minute. Add the eggplant and tomato and stir to coat with oil. Cook, stirring occasionally, until starting to soften, about 2 minutes.

3. Add the thyme, oregano, and turmeric and stir for a few seconds more, then add the barley, lentils, wine, 3½ cups (28 fl oz/825 ml) water, and ½ teaspoon salt. Cover the dish and transfer to the oven.

4. Bake, stirring halfway through, until all of the liquid is absorbed, about 1½ hours. Stir in the parsley and serve right away.

CAULIFLOWER-PUMPKIN SEED TACOS

Cauliflower is queen of the vegetable world. It has enough texture to stand in for meat, and its mellow flavor pairs well with spices and seasonings. Pepitas come from a squash grown for its large hull-less seeds, and are very different from the seeds you scrape out of a Halloween pumpkin. They require less water to grow than most nuts, and contain protein, heart-healthy fats, and plenty of vitamins and minerals.

Raw pumpkin seeds (pepitas), 1 cup (4 oz/115 g)

Cauliflower florets, 2 cups (4 oz/115 g)

Roma tomatoes, 2, chopped

Jalapeño chile, 1 large, seeded

Garlic, 3 cloves, chopped

Olive oil, 1 tablespoon

Dried sage, ½ teaspoon

Chipotle powder, ½ teaspoon

Tamari, 1 tablespoon

Sea salt

Corn tortillas, 8

Ripe avocado, 1, pitted, peeled, and cubed

Juice of ½ lime

Hot sauce, for serving (optional)

MAKES 4 SERVINGS

1. In a food processor, process the pumpkin seeds until finely ground; scrape into a small bowl and set aside. Place the cauliflower, half of the tomatoes, the jalapeño, and garlic in the processor and pulse until minced.

2. In a large sauté pan, warm the oil over medium-high heat. Add the pumpkin seeds and and cook, stirring, until lightly toasted, about 3 minutes. Scrape the cauliflower mixture into the pan with the pumpkin seeds and cook, stirring often, until the mixture is soft and browned, about 8 minutes. Add the sage, chipotle powder, tamari, and ½ teaspoon salt and stir until the pan is dry, 1–2 minutes. Transfer to a bowl.

3. In another bowl, toss together the remaining tomatoes, avocado, lime juice, and a pinch of salt.

4. To warm the tortillas, wrap in a paper towel and microwave for 2 minutes, or warm each tortilla individually by placing in a cast-iron pan over medium heat, flipping every few seconds until hot, about 1 minute.

5. Divide the filling evenly among the tortillas and top with the avocado salsa and a drizzle of hot sauce, if using. Serve right away.

BEET HUMMUS WITH SPICED
TOASTS & CASHEW CREAM

Hummus, the ubiquitous dip made from chickpeas, tahini, and lemon, can be made even more interesting with the addition of colorful vegetables like beets. The chickpeas and tahini provide lots of protein, fiber, calcium, and minerals, and beets add their own store of important vitamins and minerals. Use day-old bread for the toasts and you'll be preventing food waste as well.

FOR THE BEET HUMMUS

Beets, 8 oz (225 g), trimmed

Chickpeas, 1 can (15 oz/425 g), drained and rinsed

Garlic, 2 cloves, chopped

Tahini, ½ cup (5 oz/140 g)

Lemon juice, ½ cup (4 fl oz/120 ml)

Smoked paprika, 1 teaspoon

Sea salt

FOR THE CASHEW CREAM

Raw cashews, 1 cup (5 oz/140 g), soaked overnight

Sea salt

Add-ins such as chopped garlic, nutritional yeast, or minced fresh flat-leaf parsley (optional)

Spiced Toast Points (page 161), for serving

English cucumber, 1 large, quartered, for serving

MAKES 6 SERVINGS

1. To make the beet hummus, peel and cube the beets. Set up a steamer and steam the beets until very tender, about 10 minutes. Drain and let cool slightly.

2. In a food processor, process the beets to a purée. Add the chickpeas and garlic and process until smooth, scraping down and repeating as needed. Add the tahini and process to make a thick, smooth paste. Add the lemon juice, smoked paprika, and 1 teaspoon salt and process until well mixed. Scrape into a serving bowl or storage container. Cover and refrigerate until ready to serve.

3. To make the cashew cream, drain the cashews and place in a powerful blender or food processor. Add ½ cup (4 fl oz/120 ml) water and ½ teaspoon salt and blend, scraping down as needed, until very smooth and creamy. If desired, stir in add-ins to taste.

4. For individual servings, use salad plates. Scoop about ½ cup (4 oz/115 g) of the hummus in the center of each plate, then dollop about 3 tablespoons of the cashew cream on top. Swirl together with the back of a spoon and drizzle with oil, if desired. Place 4 toasts and some sliced cucumbers on each plate and serve right away.

TOFU & ROOT VEGETABLE SHEET PAN WITH PARSLEY PESTO

Sheet pan dinners give you a complete meal in one easy process. Tofu and vegetables are perfect on a baking sheet, soaking up seasonings as they roast. Made of soybeans, tofu can be a more sustainable protein. Like all legumes, organic soybean plants fix nitrogen in the soil, which decreases their need for chemical fertilizers.

Extra-firm tofu, 12 oz (340 g)

Extra-virgin olive oil, 2 tablespoons

Paprika, ½ teaspoon

Sea salt

Sweet potato, 10 oz (285 g), peeled and cubed or wedged

Parsnip, 8 oz (225 g), peeled and chopped

Turnip, 9 oz (250 g) cubed

Fresh rosemary, 2 tablespoons chopped

FOR THE PESTO

Fresh flat-leaf parsley leaves, 1 cup (1 oz/30 g)

Garlic, 2 cloves, chopped

Pine nuts or chopped raw cashews, ¼ cup (1¼ oz/35 g)

Sea salt

Lemon juice, 1 tablespoon

Extra-virgin olive oil, 3 tablespoons

MAKES 4–6 SERVINGS

1. Preheat the oven to 400°F (200°C). Have ready 2 rimmed baking sheets.

2. To press the tofu, drain, wrap in a thick kitchen towel, and place on a plate. Place a heavy pan or cutting board on top and let stand for about 5 minutes. Unwrap and pat dry with another towel. Transfer to a cutting board and cut into ¾-inch (2-cm) cubes.

3. Place the tofu on 1 baking sheet. Drizzle with 1 tablespoon of the oil and sprinkle with the paprika and ½ teaspoon salt. Toss gently to coat and spread evenly on the pan.

4. Place the sweet potato, parsnip, and turnip on the second baking sheet. Add the rosemary, ½ teaspoon salt, and remaining 1 tablespoon oil. Toss to coat and spread evenly on the pan. Cover the pan with foil or another pan that covers it completely to seal in the steam.

5. Roast both pans for 20 minutes. Use a metal offset spatula to flip the tofu and return to the oven for about 10 minutes more. Uncover and stir the vegetables; they should be tender and cooked through. Return to the oven, uncovered, and roast until lightly browned, about 10 minutes more. Use the spatula to scrape the contents of both pans into a serving bowl and toss to mix.

6. Meanwhile, to make the pesto, in a food processor, combine the parsley, garlic, pine nuts, and ½ teaspoon salt. Process to a smooth paste, scraping down as needed and repeating. Add the lemon juice and process, then add the oil and process again. Transfer to a small bowl.

7. Serve the roasted mixture warm, with pesto spooned over the top.

BLACK-EYED PEA CROQUETTES
WITH RÉMOULADE

Black-eyed peas are popular in the Southern United States but have been enjoyed all over the world for centuries, even in desserts. These legumes are particularly rich in folate, iron, and minerals, as well as protein, so they are an economical and flavorful way to feed a crowd. Transform them into crispy cakes with a pungent dipping sauce, and you have an irresistible meal.

Dried black-eyed peas, 1 cup (7 oz/200 g), soaked in water overnight and drained

Potatoes (such as Red Bliss or Yukon gold), 10 oz (285 g) cubed

Ground flax seeds, 1 tablespoon

Dried thyme, 1 teaspoon

Paprika, ½ teaspoon

Sea salt

Fresh flat-leaf parsley, 2 tablespoons chopped

Panko or potato flakes, ¾ cup (2¾ oz/80 g)

Olive oil, 1 tablespoon, plus more as needed

Rémoulade (page 161)

MAKES 4 SERVINGS

1. In a medium pot, combine the black-eyed peas, potatoes, and 4 cups (32 fl oz/950 ml) water. Bring to a boil, then reduce to a simmer, cover, and cook until the peas and potatoes are tender, about 45 minutes. Drain.

2. Transfer half of the pea mixture to a food processor and add the ground flax, thyme, paprika, and ½ teaspoon salt. Process until coarsely puréed, then add the remaining pea mixture and parsley and pulse a couple of times to mix. Transfer to a large bowl and stir in ½ cup (1¾ oz/50 g) of the panko. Place the remaining panko in a medium bowl.

3. Have ready a large plate or storage container for the shaped cakes. Use a ½-cup (120-ml) measure to scoop out the pea mixture, then drop each cake in the panko in the bowl. Turn to coat and press lightly to flatten to about ¾ inch (2 cm) thick. Place on the plate or in the container. Cover and refrigerate for at least 1 hour or up to 24 hour.

4. Line a large plate with paper towels. Heat a large frying pan over medium-high heat for 1 minute, then drizzle in the oil. Place half of the cakes in the hot oil and cook, reducing the heat to medium as the cakes start to sizzle, until they are golden brown on both sides, 3–4 minutes per side. Drain on paper towels. Repeat to cook the remaining cakes, adding more oil as needed. Serve right away with the rémoulade.

MUSHROOM-WALNUT LOAF
WITH HERBED STREUSEL

Meat loaf is comfort food for many people, and this vegan version will satisy you in all the right ways. Ground walnuts, sunflower seeds, pumpkin seeds, and oats combine with minced mushrooms to create a meatlike texture. Seeds are nutritious, sustainable, and inexpensive and add depth of flavor to the mix.

Yellow onion, 1 peeled

Olive oil, 1 tablespoon

Button mushrooms, 8 oz (225 g), trimmed and coarsely chopped

Garlic, 3 cloves, chopped

Rolled oats, 1 cup (3 oz/90 g)

Walnuts, 1 cup (4 oz/115 g)

Raw sunflower seeds and raw pumpkin seeds (pepitas), ½ cup (2 oz/60 g) *each*

Black beans, 1 can (15 oz/425 g), drained and rinsed

Ground flax seeds, ¼ cup (¾ oz/26 g)

Tamari, 2 tablespoons

Tomato paste, 2 tablespoons

Vegan mustard, 1 tablespoon

Dried thyme and dried sage, 1 teaspoon *each*

Freshly ground pepper

FOR THE STREUSEL

Rolled oats, 3 tablespoons

Whole-wheat flour, 1 tablespoon

Dried oregano, 1 teaspoon

Sea salt

Avocado oil, 2 teaspoons

1. Preheat the oven to 375°F (190°C). Lightly oil a 9-by-5-by-3-inch (23-by-13-by-7.5-cm) loaf pan.

2. In a food processor, process the onion until minced. In a large frying pan, warm the olive oil over medium-high heat. Scrape the onion into the pan and cook, stirring occasionally, until softened, about 5 minutes. Place the mushrooms in the processor and pulse until minced, then scrape into the pan. Cook until the mushrooms are shrunken and browned and the pan is nearly dry, about 5 minutes. Add the garlic and cook, stirring, until fragrant, about 1 minute. Transfer the mushroom mixture to a large bowl and let cool.

3. Wipe out the processor bowl and add the oats, walnuts, sunflower seeds, and pumpkin seeds. Pulse on and off to mince to the size of ground beef. Add the beans and pulse just to coarsely chop the beans, not purée.

4. Transfer the bean mixture to the bowl with the mushroom mixture. Add the ground flax, tamari, tomato paste, mustard, thyme, sage, and ½ teaspoon pepper. Use your hands to mix until well combined and then press into the prepared pan. Smooth the top.

5. To make the streusel, in a small bowl, stir together the oats, flour, oregano, ¼ teaspoon salt, and the avocado oil. Sprinkle over the loaf and press to adhere.

6. Bake until the top is golden brown and the loaf feels firm when pressed, about 45 minutes. Cool in the pan for 10 minutes before cutting and serving. The loaf can be stored, tightly covered in the refrigerator, for up to 4 days.

MAKES 8 SERVINGS

ROASTED VEGETABLE, HAZELNUT & HERB STRUDEL

Around the holidays, cooks begin looking for a centerpiece dish. This burnished, flaky strudel fits the bill, with an appealing filo crust filled with tender, richly caramelized vegetables. Hazelnuts provide crunch and protein and are one of the nuts that requires very little water to grow. Olive oil yields a more tender crust; if you prefer, substitute coconut oil to make it crisper.

Olive oil, 3 tablespoons

Yellow onions, 3 large, chopped

Parsnips, 2, peeled and cubed

Butternut squash, peeled, seeded, and cubed

Turnip, 1 large, quartered or cubed

Fresh sage, 1 tablespoon chopped

Fresh thyme, 1 tablespoon chopped

Sea salt and freshly ground pepper

Fresh flat-leaf parsley, ½ cup (¾ oz/20 g) chopped

Hazelnuts, ½ cup (2½ oz/70 g), toasted, skinned, and coarsely chopped

FOR THE STRUDEL

Olive oil or melted coconut oil, ¼ cup (2 fl oz/60 ml)

Filo dough, 6 sheets, thawed

MAKES 4–6 SERVINGS

1. One or two hours before you will assemble the strudel, in a large sauté pan, warm 2 tablespoons of the oil over medium heat. Add the onions and bring to a sizzle, stirring to coat, then reduce the heat to medium-low and and cook, stirring every 10 minutes or so, until the onions have reduced in volume and are caramel brown, 45–60 minutes.

2. Preheat the oven to 400°F (200°C).

3. Combine the parsnips, squash, and turnip in a large roasting pan and drizzle with the remaining 1 tablespoon oil. Add the sage, thyme, 1 teaspoon salt, and ½ teaspoon pepper and toss to coat. Cover the pan with foil or another pan that covers it completely and roast for 25 minutes. Uncover and stir, then cover again and roast until tender and lightly browned, about 20 minutes more. Let cool to room temperature, then stir in the parsley and hazelnuts. Set aside.

4. To make the strudel, use a pastry brush to brush a baking dish or rimmed baking sheet with some of the ¼ cup (2 fl oz/60 ml) oil. Place a sheet of filo on the pan and brush the filo with some of the oil. Stack another sheet on top, and repeat until all 6 sheets are oiled and stacked.

* Continued on following page

4. Place the vegetable filling in the center of the dough, using a spatula to form a 10-by-6-inch (25-by-15-cm) rectangle in the middle with a border of about 4 inches (10 cm) of filo on all sides. Shape the filling evenly, then fold in the short sides, then the longer sides, and then carefully turn the strudel over. Brush the top with more oil. Use a paring knife to cut about 6 slits across the top for steam to escape.

5. Bake until the top is crisp and golden, about 25 minutes. Serve warm.

Recipe note

Always thaw filo dough in the refrigerator overnight, or for at least 4 hours, or it can turn out brittle or soggy. This recipe calls for standard whole sheets (18 by 14 inches/45 by 35 cm), but if you buy smaller ones, just overlap two to make a layer the same size as a large sheet.

SWEET POTATO FRIES
WITH LENTIL-GARLIC HUMMUS

Everyone loves fries, so why not make a colorful fiber- and antioxidant-rich version from sweet potatoes? Instead of dipping them in ketchup, serve them with a garlicky, nutty red lentil hummus with enough protein to make it a meal. Red lentils vary in size and cooking time, so just keep tabs on their progress and cook them until they are tender but not falling apart.

FOR THE HUMMUS

Dried red lentils, 1 cup (7 oz/200 g), picked over and rinsed

Garlic, 6 cloves

Tahini, ½ cup (5 oz/140 g)

Sea salt

Lemon juice, 6 tablespoons

FOR THE FRIES

Sweet potato, 1 large, cut into strips ½ inch (12 mm) wide

Olive oil, 2 tablespoons

Paprika, 1 teaspoon

Coarse salt

MAKES 4–6 SERVINGS

1. To make the hummus, in a small pot, combine the lentils, garlic, and 2 cups (16 fl oz/475 ml) water and bring to a boil over high heat. Reduce the heat to maintain a gentle simmer and cook until the lentils are very soft, 15–20 minutes. Drain in a wire mesh strainer; do not rinse.

2. Transfer the lentils and garlic to a food processor. Process until puréed, scraping down as needed to make a smooth paste. Add the tahini and ¾ teaspoon sea salt and process until smooth. Add the lemon juice and process to mix. Transfer to a bowl or storage container.

3. To make the fries, preheat the oven to 400°F (200°C).

4. Place the sweet potato strips on a rimmed baking sheet. Drizzle with the oil, sprinkle with the paprika and ½ teaspoon coarse salt, and toss to coat. Roast until tender when pierced with a paring knife, about 20 minutes. Let cool slightly, then serve the fries with the hummus.

Recipe note

Supermarket shelves are packed with hummus products, but nothing beats homemade hummus. Plus, it's easy to prepare! Chickpeas, an inexpensive source of protein, are the base for classic hummus, but there are endless riffs on the traditional recipe; beets, lentils, and sweet potatoes are three popular substitutes for chickpeas.

TEMPEH CUTLETS IN HERB SAUCE WITH CAPERS

Tempeh is often prepared with Indonesian and other Asian flavors, but it is equally tasty with other seasonings. In this French-inspired dish, a thin slice of tempeh is bathed in a rosemary-infused sauce. It's delicious over rice or noodles—and it doesn't hurt that organic soy foods can help shrink your carbon footprint.

Tempeh, 8 oz (225 g)

Vegan white wine, ¾ cup
(6 fl oz/180 ml)

Garlic, 2 cloves, crushed

Herbes de Provence, 1 tablespoon

Sea salt and freshly ground pepper

Cherry tomatoes, 1 cup (6 oz/170 g), halved

Green olives, ¼ cup (1 oz/30 g), pitted and halved

Capers, 2 tablespoons, rinsed and drained

Tomato paste, 1 tablespoon

Organic sugar

Extra-virgin olive oil, 1 tablespoon

Fresh basil, ½ cup (¾ oz/20 g) chopped, plus sprigs for garnish (optional)

MAKES 2 SERVINGS

1. Using a chef's knife, cut the tempeh into 2 thin slabs using a chef's knife. Place in a ceramic or stainless-steel pan large enough to hold both pieces. In a small saucepan, stir together the wine, garlic, herbes de Provence, ½ teaspoon salt, and a few grinds of pepper and bring to a boil over high heat. Pour over the tempeh and cover. Refrigerate overnight.

2. In a medium bowl, stir together the tomatoes, olives, capers, tomato paste, ¼ teaspoon salt, and a pinch of sugar.

3. Remove the marinated tempeh from the refrigerator. Remove the slices from the marinade and place on a plate, reserving the marinade.

4. In a large sauté pan, warm the oil over medium-high heat. Place the tempeh slices in the pan and cook until browned, about 2 minutes per side. Transfer to a plate. Pour the reserved marinade into the pan. Bring to a boil and add the tomato mixture. Boil until the tomatoes are softened and the pan is nearly dry, about 5 minutes. Stir in the basil just before serving.

5. Place each tempeh cutlet on a plate and top with sauce. Garnish with basil sprigs, if desired, and serve right away.

RED BEANS & RICE WITH BRAISED COLLARDS & SMOKED ALMONDS

Eating plant-based meals made in a slow-simmering single pot with low-cost ingredients is a win-win-win and helped make red beans and rice a Southern staple. In this rendition, you'll use brown rice for its beneficial fiber and minerals, and add some stewed collard greens to round out the dish. A sprinkling of smoked almonds lends crunch and the smoky flavor which is iconic in the traditional version.

Long-grain brown rice, 1 cup (7 oz/200 g)

Extra-virgin olive oil, 2 tablespoons

Yellow onion, 1 small, chopped

Red bell pepper, 1 large, seeded and chopped

Garlic, 2 cloves, chopped

Jalapeño chile, 1 small, seeded and chopped

Dried sage, 1 teaspoon

Sea salt

Dried red beans, 1 cup (7 oz/200 g), soaked overnight and drained

Green onions, 4, chopped

Fresh flat-leaf parsley, ½ cup (¾ oz/20 g) chopped

Collard greens, 1 bunch, stemmed; ribs and leaves chopped separately

Roma tomato, 1 large, chopped

Vegetable broth or water, ½ cup (4 fl oz/120 ml), plus more as needed

Paprika, ½ teaspoon

Smoked almonds, ½ cup (2 oz/60 g), coarsely chopped

MAKES 4–6 SERVINGS

1. Place 2 cups (16 fl oz/475 ml) water in a saucepan and bring to a boil. Add the rice and return to a boil, then cover tightly, reduce the heat to low, and cook until all of the water is absorbed, about 40 minutes. Uncover, fluff the rice with a fork, re-cover, and let stand for at least 5 minutes.

2. In a large pot, warm 1 tablespoon of the oil over medium-high heat. Add the onion, bell pepper, and garlic and cook, stirring, until starting to soften, about 5 minutes. Reduce the heat to medium, add the jalapeño, sage, and ½ teaspoon salt, and cook until fragrant, about 5 minutes. Add 3 cups (24 fl oz/700 ml) water and the beans, raise the heat to high, and bring to a boil. Cover, reduce the heat to medium-low, and simmer gently until the beans are very tender, about 1 hour. Uncover and stir in the green onions and parsley. Keep warm.

3. In a large sauté pan, warm the remaining 1 tablespoon oil over medium-high heat. Add the collard ribs and cook, stirring occasionally, until starting to soften, about 4 minutes. Add the collard leaves and tomato and cook, stirring occasionally, until the leaves start to soften, about 3 minutes. Add the broth, paprika, and ½ teaspoon salt and bring to a boil. Reduce the heat to maintain a simmer and cook to your preferred level of doneness, adding more broth as needed.

4. To serve, place a mound of rice in each bowl. Top with the beans, greens, and smoked almonds. Serve right away.

GUMBO Z'HERBES WITH MILLET

A big pot of green goodness, gumbo z'herbes is made by stewing and then puréeing hearty collards, spicy mustard greens, and peppery watercress. All those sustainable greens provide vitamins and minerals and even some protein. You'll need to add gumbo filé, an herbal powder made with ground sassafras leaves. The seasoning is a traditional mixture created by the Choctaw Indigenous peoples of the Southern U.S.

Extra-virgin olive oil, 6 tablespoons (3 fl oz/90 ml)

Leeks, 2–3 large, white and pale green parts, sliced

Celery, 1 cup (5 oz/140 g) chopped

Green onions, 4 large, chopped

Fresh flat-leaf parsley, ½ cup (¾ oz/20 g) chopped

Garlic cloves, 4 large, chopped

Filé powder, 1 tablespoon

Dried oregano, ½ teaspoon

Chipotle powder, ½ teaspoon

Cayenne pepper, ¼ teaspoon

Collard greens, 4 cups sliced leaves, stems chopped

Mustard greens, 4 cups sliced

Watercress or arugula, 2 cups loosely packed

Organic sugar

Vegetable broth, 5 cups (40 fl oz/1.2 l)

All-purpose flour, ¼ cup (1 oz/30 g)

Sea salt and freshly ground pepper

Millet, 1½ cups (12 oz/340 g)

MAKES 6 SERVINGS

1. In a very large pot, warm 2 tablespoons of the oil over medium-high heat. Add the leeks and celery and cook, stirring, until they sizzle. Reduce the heat to medium-low and stir frequently until the vegetables are soft, about 8 minutes. Add the green onions, parsley, and garlic and and cook, stirring, until the onions wilt, 2–3 minutes. Add the filé powder, oregano, chipotle powder, and cayenne and stir until fragrant, about 3 minutes. Add the collard greens and chopped stems, mustard greens, watercress, and a pinch of sugar, and toss to combine. Add 2 cups (16 fl oz/475 ml) of the broth. Cover and cook, stirring occasionally, until the greens are tender, about 15 minutes. Remove from the heat.

2. In a food processor, working in batches, purée the greens, scraping down the sides as needed. Transfer to a bowl. Rinse and dry the pot.

3. In the same pot, warm the remaining ¼ cup (2 fl oz/60 ml) oil over medium-high heat. Add the flour and whisk until smooth. When it starts to bubble, reduce the heat to keep the mixture at a gentle simmer. Cook, whisking often, until the roux is the color of peanut butter, about 7 minutes. Whisk in the remaining 3 cups (24 fl oz/700 ml) broth and bring to a boil. Stir in the puréed greens. Simmer the gumbo for 10 minutes to blend the flavors. Season to taste with salt and pepper. Keep warm.

4. In a small pot, toast the millet over medium-high heat until the grains start to smell like popcorn. Remove from the heat. Add 3 cups (24 fl oz/700 ml) water and 1 teaspoon salt. Return the pot to high heat and bring to a boil. Cover tightly, reduce the heat to low, and simmer until tender, about 15 minutes. Fluff and let stand, covered, to steam, about 5 minutes.

5. Divide the millet among bowls and spoon the gumbo on top. Serve right away.

RICE WITH CHIPOTLE & KIDNEY BEANS

Inspired by the hearty peas-and-rice dish originating in South Carolina in the U.S., this classic recipe uses kidney beans in place of the traditional black-eyed peas. The addition of smoky paprika and chipotle give it a lovely richness, and healthful olive oil bolsters the complexity. Add some sautéed green peppers if you'd like, or serve with a side of corn bread and collard greens.

Extra-virgin olive oil, 2 tablespoons

Garlic, 4 cloves, chopped

Dried or fresh thyme, 1 teaspoon

Chipotle powder, ½ teaspoon

Smoked paprika, ½ teaspoon

Bay leaf, 1

Basmati rice or jasmine rice, 1½ cups (10½ oz/300 g)

Sea salt

Cooked kidney beans, 1 cup (7 oz/200 g), drained and rinsed

Green onions, 4 large, thinly sliced

Fresh flat-leaf parsley, ½ cup (¾ oz/20 g) chopped

MAKES 4–6 SERVINGS

1. In a large pot, warm the oil over medium-high heat. Add the garlic and stir until it starts to sizzle, about 1 minute, then reduce the heat to low. Add the thyme, chipotle powder, paprika, and bay leaf and stir until fragrant, about 1 minute.

2. Add 2¼ cups (18 fl oz/525 ml) water, raise the heat to high, and bring to a boil. Add the rice and ½ teaspoon salt and return to a boil. Cover tightly, reduce the heat to low, and cook until all of the water is absorbed, about 15 minutes. Fold in the beans, green onions, and parsley and serve right away.

THE QUEST FOR PLANT-BASED PROTEIN

Plant-based protein is not recent or absent in the global human diet. Tofu, a source of protein made from soybean curd, has been a staple in China since the Song dynasty thousands of years ago.[1] Over the next several centuries, the production and consumption of tofu spread to other Asian countries—Japan, Vietnam, parts of Southeast Asia—and beyond. In the United States, one of the earliest mentions of tofu was in a letter written by Benjamin Franklin in the late eighteenth century. About one hundred years later, the first U.S. tofu company, Wo Sing & Co., in San Francisco was established.[2]

Another source of plant-based protein, wheat gluten, has been documented in China since the sixth century.[3] Also known as seitan, it is made by washing wheat flour dough until all the starch is removed, leaving behind an insoluble gluten that is then cooked before serving, typically as an ingredient in noodles or as a meat substitute. This found its way to Europe in the eighteenth century and was first discussed in De Frumento, an Italian treatise on wheat that relayed Jacopo Bartolomeo Beccari's finding of gluten in wheat flour.[4]

For many societies, staple, protein-rich plant-based foods have long been part of their culture, such as quinoa in Peru, Bolivia, and Chile. In the Americas, Indigenous peoples long had heavily plant-based diets, though the trend across European and American societies in search for alternative proteins took off in the mid-nineteenth and the beginning of the twentieth centuries.[5]

[1] Shurtleff, William, H T Huang, and Akiko Aoyagi. 2014. History of Soybeans and Soyfoods in China and Taiwan, and in Chinese Cookbooks, Restaurants, and Chinese Work with Soyfoods Outside China (1024 BCE to 2014) Extensively Annotated Bibliography and Sourcebook: Including Manchuria, Hong Kong and Tibet. Lafayette, Ca Soyinfo Center.
[2] Shurtleff, Huang, and Aoyagi, History of Soybeans and Soyfoods, 6.
[3] Ibid, 2478–2479.
[4] Pini, Giovanni. 1940. Jacopo Bartolomeo Beccari. Cappelli.
[5] Miller, Laura J. 2017. Building Nature's Market: The Business and Politics of Natural Foods. University of Chicago Press. p. 30.

As societies become increasingly concerned with the carbon footprint of animal-agriculture and the factory farms that produce animal products, *the demand for a diverse array of plant-based proteins has ignited a shift in our food system.* All veggies have protein and the benefit of so many other essential nutrients. When we open our minds, we can find nutrition and easy to digest foods in so many more places than we ever thought. For many companies, the race is on to bring products that capture the taste, texture, and mouthfeel of animal-based protein to the dinner table while reducing the world's carbon footprint. By simply increasing the variety of plant-based foods in our diets, we increase the diversity of protein sources.

Though the path to a diverse array of plant-based proteins varies greatly, *at the heart of this quest lies the key to environmental sustainability: science and technology, united with human tradition and creativity.*

DESSERTS

"Just as people can share seeds, so too can we share nature's bounty with one another." —Jane

AQUAFABA CHOCOLATE MOUSSE

For years, we opened our cans of chickpeas and poured the liquid down the drain. Then we found out that the liquid we were discarding could be substituted for egg whites! It was named "aquafaba" and a new plant-based ingredient was born. This chocolate mousse transforms a bit of lush dark chocolate into an elegant dessert by harnessing the magic of the bean cooking liquid that we used to throw away.

Semisweet nondairy chocolate (not chips), 4 oz (115 g), chopped

Aquafaba, ½ cup (4 fl oz/120 ml)

Cream of tartar, ¼ teaspoon

Organic sugar, 3 tablespoons

Seasonal fresh fruit, such as sliced pitted cherries, berries, orange segments, or sliced pears, for garnish

MAKES 4 SERVINGS

1. In a double boiler or in the microwave, melt the chocolate. Cool to room temperature.

2. In a stand mixer with the whisk attachment, or in a large bowl with an electric mixer, combine the aquafaba and cream of tartar. Mix on low speed until combined. Raise the speed to high and beat until the mixture forms firm peaks, about 10 minutes. Sprinkle in 1 tablespoon of the sugar and beat for 2 minutes, then sprinkle in the remaining 1 tablespoon sugar and beat for 2 minutes more.

3. Drizzle the cooled melted chocolate over the aquafaba mixture and use a rubber spatula to gently fold in the chocolate. The mixture will deflate quite a bit but stay fluffy. Transfer to jars, dessert bowls, or a storage container and refrigerate until set, about 30 minutes. Garnish the mousse with the fruit and serve.

BANANA-COCONUT & ROSEMARY NICE CREAM

If ice cream is your weakness, get ready for nice cream. Frozen bananas are the secret ingredient here, puréed and then blended with rosemary-infused coconut milk. It will ring all the bells that ice cream would, with none of the dairy fat or cholesterol. When you have bananas on the counter that have gotten overly ripe, just slice and freeze them, and you'll be ready to make nice cream.

Overripe or ripe bananas, 10, peeled and cut into ½-inch (12-mm)

Canned coconut milk, 1½ cups (12 fl oz/350 ml)

Fresh rosemary, 6 small sprigs

Agave nectar, 2 tablespoons

Toasted flaked coconut, ½ cup (1½ oz/40 g)

MAKES 4 SERVINGS

1. Line 2 rimmed baking sheets with parchment paper. Place the banana slices on the prepared baking sheets and cover. Freeze overnight or until firm.

2. In a small saucepan, combine the coconut milk, 2 of the rosemary sprigs, and agave nectar over medium-low heat. Bring to a simmer and simmer gently for 5 minutes. Remove the pan from the heat, cover, and let stand for at least 20 minutes to allow the flavors to infuse. Remove the rosemary sprigs and discard 1 sprig. Pick the leaves from the other sprig and reserve.

3. In a powerful blender, blend the frozen bananas until very finely chopped. Add ⅔ cup (5½ fl oz/160 ml) of the coconut milk mixture and the reserved rosemary leaves. Blend until the mixture forms a soft-serve ice-cream texture, scraping down the sides as needed.

4. Spoon the banana mixture into glasses or bowls and drizzle with the remaining coconut milk mixture. Top with the coconut flakes and remaining 4 rosemary sprigs and serve right away.

Recipe notes

Bananas should be ripe for the best flavor and texture.

The texture of the nice cream is best as soon as it is made, but it can be frozen for up to 2 days.

CHOCOLATE NO-CHURN NICE CREAM

You don't need an ice cream maker to make an amazing plant-based ice cream. Thanks to "aquafaba," you can create the texture of churned cream, without cream. Aquafaba is the liquid you drain from canned chickpeas, and it has the unique ability to hold a lofty, whipped structure that keeps the creamy mixture from being too dense. The amount of cream in each brand of canned coconut milk will be slightly different; freeze any extra from your can.

Coconut cream, 1 cup
(8 fl oz/240 g)

Refined coconut oil, ¼ cup
(2 fl oz/60 ml) melted

Unsweetened cocoa powder,
½ cup (1½ oz/40 g)

Aquafaba, ¼ cup (2 fl oz/60 ml)

Cream of tartar, ¼ teaspoon

Vanilla extract, 1 teaspoon

Organic powdered sugar, 1 cup
(4 oz/115 g)

MAKES 4 SERVINGS

1. Have ready a 9-by-5-by-3-inch (23-by-13-by-7.5-cm) loaf pan or a 4-cup (32 fl oz/950 ml) storage container.

2. In a medium bowl, whisk together the coconut cream and coconut oil until combined. Sift the cocoa over the bowl and whisk until well combined, making sure there are no lumps.

3. In a stand mixer with the whisk attachment, or in a large bowl with an electric mixer, combine the aquafaba and cream of tartar. Mix on low speed until combined. Add the vanilla, raise the speed to high, and beat until very fluffy and white, about 6 minutes. With the mixer running on medium speed, add the powdered sugar ¼ cup (1 oz/30 g) at a time, sprinkling it in gradually, and beat until well combined and fluffy.

4. Using a spatula, fold the coconut mixture into the aquafaba mixture until smooth but not deflated. If there are lumps, smash them with the spatula. Transfer to the loaf pan and smooth the top. Cover tightly and freeze for at least 3 hours or up to 2 weeks.

5. Let stand at room temperature for a few minutes to soften, then use an ice-cream scoop dipped in warm water to scoop. Serve right away.

TAPIOCA PUDDING
WITH TROPICAL FRUITS

Pearl tapioca is a gluten-free starch, and making pudding with it couldn't be easier. In this recipe, a bit of coconut milk contributes richness, and the juicy tropical fruits add an appealing sweet-tart note. Both mango and papaya are high in vitamins C and A and are antioxidant rich. You can also use other fruits in season, like berries or peaches.

Small pearl tapioca, ½ cup
(3 oz/90 g)

Coconut milk, ¼ cup (2 fl oz/60 ml)

Organic sugar, 2 tablespoons

Ripe mango, 1, peeled, pitted, and diced

Ripe papaya, ½, peeled, seeded, and sliced

1 lime, juiced

Turbinado sugar, 4 teaspoons

MAKES 4–6 SERVINGS

1. In a saucepan, bring 4 cups (32 fl oz/950 ml) water to a boil over high heat. Reduce the heat to medium, add the tapioca, and simmer gently until translucent, 12–15 minutes. Drain thoroughly through a fine-mesh sieve.

2. Transfer the tapioca to a bowl. Add the coconut milk and organic sugar and stir until the sugar is dissolved. Cover and refrigerate until well chilled, at least 1 hour or up to 24 hours.

3. Divide the pudding among dessert bowls and top with the mango and papya. Drizzle with the lime juice, sprinkle with the turbinado sugar, and serve right away.

CANDIED ORANGE PEEL DIPPED IN CHOCOLATE

Eating oranges boosts immunity, and repurposing the peels into a delicious candy makes good use of waste. Don't be intimidated by working with sugar. These treats are quite easy to make, as all you need are sugar and orange peel—and a bit of patience. Dipping the peel in nondairy dark chocolate adds lusciousness as well as a coating that's rich in antioxidants.

Organic navel oranges, 2 large

Organic sugar, 2 cups (14 oz/400 g)

Turbinado sugar, ½ cup (3½ oz/105 g)

Semisweet nondairy chocolate, 8 oz (225 g)

MAKES ABOUT 45 CANDIES

1. Bring a saucepan of water to a boil. Cut a ½-inch (12-mm) slice from the top and bottom of each orange to make flat surfaces. Cut the remaining peel on each orange into 4 vertical segments. Remove each section of peel in 1 piece. (Reserve the oranges for another use.) Lay the peel flat on a cutting board and use a chef's knife to cut into strips ¼ inch (6 mm) wide. Drop the strips in the pan and cook until starting to soften, about 15 minutes. Drain, rinse, and drain again.

2. In the same saucepan, combine the organic sugar and 2 cups (16 fl oz/475 ml) water and bring to a boil, stirring to dissolve the sugar. Add the peel and return to a boil. Reduce the heat and simmer until the peel is very soft, about 45 minutes. Drain, reserving the sugar syrup for another use.

3. On a rimmed baking sheet, toss the peel and the turbinado sugar, separating the strips. Lift the peel from the sugar and transfer it to a sheet of foil. Let stand until the coating is dry, 1–2 days.

4. Line a rimmed baking sheet with parchment paper. In a double boiler or in the microwave, melt the chocolate. Dip each dried strip in the chocolate, covering about half of each one. Place the strips on the prepared pan as you go. Let the chocolate set for about 1 hour, then serve. The candies can be stored, tightly covered in the refrigerator, for up to 1 week.

APPLE CRANBERRY CRUMBLE BARS

Full of whole-grain goodness and healthful fruit, these chewy, oaty bars are a treat you can feel good about. Cranberries are especially high in antioxidants and vitamin C, so don't just enjoy them at Thanksgiving. They are available frozen, year-round, and you can easily freeze your own on rimmed baking sheets and transfer to freezer bags when solid. If using frozen berries, increase the baking time by a few minutes.

Coconut oil, 1 tablespoon

Sweet baking apples (such as Gala or Golden Delicious), 6, peeled, cored, and sliced (1 lb/450 g)

Fresh or frozen cranberries, 1 cup (4 oz/115 g)

Brown sugar, ½ cup (3½ oz/100 g) firmly packed

Vanilla extract, 1 teaspoon

FOR THE CRUMBLE

Rolled oats, 2 cups (6 oz/170 g)

All-purpose flour, 2 cups (9 oz/250 g)

Brown sugar, 1 cup (7½ oz/210 g) firmly packed

Baking soda, 1 teaspoon

Sea salt

Coconut oil, ½ cup (4 fl oz/120 ml) melted

Unsweetened nondairy milk, ½ cup (4 fl oz/120 ml)

Ground cinnamon, 1 teaspoon

MAKES 16–20 BARS

1. Preheat the oven to 350°F (180°C). Grease a 9-by-13-inch (23-by-33-cm) baking pan.

2. In a saucepan, warm the oil over low heat. Add the apples and cook, stirring often, until starting to soften, about 5 minutes. Add the cranberries and stir just until a few berries pop, about 2 minutes. Sprinkle in the brown sugar and vanilla and cook, stirring, until the mixture is melted and syrupy, 2–3 minutes. Remove from the heat.

3. To make the crumble, in a large bowl, stir together the oats, flour, brown sugar, baking soda, and ¼ teaspoon salt. Drizzle in the oil and nondairy milk and stir until the mixture holds its shape when squeezed. Sprinkle half of the mixture over the bottom of the prepared pan. Dampen your hands and press the crumble into the pan, dampening again as needed to keep the mixture from sticking to your hands.

4. Add the cinnamon to the remaining oat mixture and toss to mix. Spread the apple mixture in the pan and crumble the remaining oat mixture over it evenly. Press gently with the palms of your hands to make even bars.

5. Bake until the top is firm to the touch and the edges are golden brown, 30–35 minutes. Cool completely in the pan on a rack and then refrigerate until cold. Cut into squares and serve. Or just eat warm and messy. The bars can be stored, tightly covered in the refrigerator, for up to 1 week.

BANANA-CHOCOLATE CHIP CUPCAKES

Save those overripe bananas and the liquid from canned chickpeas in the freezer, and you will always be ready to whip up these delectable cupcakes with just a few pantry ingredients. These cupcakes will make your day—share them to make someone else's!

All-purpose flour, 1¼ cups (5½ oz/155 g)

Baking powder, 1 teaspoon

Sea salt

Overripe bananas, 2, peeled

Organic sugar, ¾ cup (5 oz/140 g)

Aquafaba, ¾ cup (6 oz/180 ml)

Avocado oil, ¼ cup (2 fl oz/60 ml)

Vanilla extract, 1 teaspoon

Semisweet nondairy chocolate chips, 1 cup (6 oz/170 g)

FOR THE GANACHE

Semisweet nondairy chocolate, 3 oz (90 g), chopped

Coconut milk, ¼ cup (2 fl oz/60 ml)

MAKES 12 CUPCAKES

1. Preheat the oven to 350°F (180°C). Line 12 standard muffin cups with paper liners.

2. In a large bowl, whisk together the flour, baking powder, and ½ teaspoon salt. Set aside.

3. In a food processor, process the bananas until smooth, scraping down and processing again to make sure all of the bits are puréed. With the machine running, pour the sugar through the feed tube, and when combined, pour in the aquafaba. Process until the mixture is light and pale, about 2 minutes. With the machine running, drizzle in the oil and vanilla, stopping as soon as they are mixed in. Pour the aquafaba mixture over the flour mixture and fold in just until mixed and then quickly fold in the chocolate chips.

4. Use a ⅓-cup (80-ml) measure to scoop the batter into the prepared muffin cups, dividing any leftover batter among them.

5. Bake until a toothpick inserted into a cupcake in the middle of the pan comes out with only a few moist crumbs attached, about 20 minutes..

6. Cool the cupcakes in the pan on a rack for 10 minutes, then transfer the cakes to the rack to cool completely.

7. Meanwhile, to make the ganache, combine the chocolate and coconut milk in a double boiler and stir until smooth. Let cool slightly, then dip the top of each cooled cupcake in the ganache and transfer to a rack or platter. When the ganache has set, about 30 minutes, serve. The cupcakes can be stored, tightly covered in the refrigerator, for up to 4 days.

OAT, SEED & PEANUT BUTTER SNACK COOKIES

If you like the chewiness of an oatmeal cookie, you will love this oaty, chunky, maple-sweet wonder. Instead of the empty calories of a sugary white-flour cookie, this one delivers real food, and makes a respectable breakfast or snack that feels like a treat. Crunchy sunflower or pumpkin seeds are often overlooked in baking, but they are a sustainable, healthful alternative to nuts and contain protein, fiber, and good fats.

Rolled oats, 1 cup (3 oz/90 g)

Whole-wheat pastry flour, 1 cup (4 oz/115 g)

Ground cinnamon, 1 teaspoon

Baking soda, ½ teaspoon

Sea salt

Maple syrup, ½ cup (5½ oz/155 g)

Smooth unsweetened peanut butter, ½ cup (5 oz/140 g)

Unsweetened nondairy milk, ¼ cup (2 fl oz/60 ml)

Avocado oil, ¼ cup (2 fl oz/60 ml)

Ground flax seeds, 2 tablespoons

Vanilla extract, ½ teaspoon

Raisins or other chopped dried fruit, ½ cup (3 oz/90 g)

Sunflower seeds or raw pumpkin seeds (pepitas), ½ cup (2 oz/60 g)

MAKES 4 COOKIES

1. Preheat the oven to 350°F (180°C). Lightly oil 2 rimmed baking sheets or line them with parchment paper.

2. In a large bowl, stir together the oats, flour, cinnamon, baking soda, and ½ teaspoon salt. In a medium bowl, stir together the maple syrup, peanut butter, nondairy milk, oil, ground flax, and vanilla. Stir the maple syrup mixture into the oat mixture until well combined, then stir in the raisins and seeds.

3. Scoop ¼-cup (60-g) portions of dough and place on the prepared baking sheets. Flatten each cookie with a dampened palm to about ½ inch (12 mm) thick. Bake for 8 minutes, then flip the cookies and bake until they look dry on the surface (they will still seem soft), about 8 minutes more. The cookies will seem soft but look dry on the surface. Cool on the pans until firm enough to remove with a spatula, then transfer to racks. Serve warm or at room temperature. The cookies can be stored, tightly covered at room temperature, for up to 1 week.

TAHINI & CHOCOLATE CHUNK COOKIES

Peanut butter and nondairy chocolate are a well-known pair but tahini makes a smooth and delicious partner for chocolate, too. Either the traditional, pourable style of tahini or the thicker, more coarsely ground style works here—your cookies will spread less with the latter. Tahini is an excellent source of plant-based protein and calcium.

All-purpose flour, 1 cup (4 oz/115 g)

Arrowroot, 2 tablespoons

Baking soda, ½ teaspoon

Sea salt

Unsweetened nondairy milk, ¼ cup (2 fl oz/60 ml)

Ground flax seeds, 1 tablespoon

Refined coconut oil, ½ cup (4 fl oz/120 ml), melted

Tahini, ½ cup (5 oz/140 g)

Brown sugar, 1 cup (7½ oz/210 g) firmly packed

Dark nondairy chocolate, 6 oz (170 g) chopped

Sesame seeds, 2 tablespoons

MAKES 12 COOKIES

1. In a medium bowl, whisk together the flour, arrowroot, baking soda, and ½ teaspoon salt. In a small bowl, stir together the nondairy milk and ground flax and let stand for 5 minutes for the flax to gel.

2. In a stand mixer with the whisk attachment, or in a large bowl with an electric mixer, beat the coconut oil and tahini until smooth. Mix in the brown sugar until smooth. Scrape the thickened flax into the tahini mixture and beat until smooth. On low speed, add the flour mixture and beat until just mixed in, then add the chocolate just until combined. Refrigerate the dough for 30 minutes.

3. Preheat the oven to 350°F (180°C). Line 2 rimmed baking sheets with parchment paper.

4. Use scant ¼-cup (60-g) portions of dough to form balls and place 6 balls on each prepared baking sheet with 2 inches (5 cm) between the cookies. Flatten each ball with a dampened palm to about ¾ inch (2 cm) thick. Sprinkle about ½ teaspoon sesame seeds on each cookie.

5. Bake until the cookies are browned on the edges and firm on top, about 15 minutes, reversing the positions of the pans halfway. Cool on racks for about 5 minutes, then use a spatula to transfer the cookies to the racks. Serve warm or at room temperarure. The cookies can be stored, tightly covered at room temperature, for up to 4 days.

MOCHA BROWNIES

With a decadent coffee-infused frosting and a layer of deep, dark ganache, these brownies are impressive and indulgent. Organic cocoa and nondairy chocolate are best, and look for chocolate that is also labeled Fair Trade to support companies that compensate their workers adequately and have good labor conditions internationally.

FOR THE BROWNIES

All-purpose flour, 1½ cups
(6½ oz/185 g)

Unsweetened cocoa powder,
¾ cup (2¼ oz/65 g)

Organic sugar, ¾ cup (5 oz/140 g)

Arrowroot, 2 tablespoons

Baking powder, 1 teaspoon

Sea salt

Maple syrup, ½ cup (5½ oz/155 g)

Coconut milk, ½ cup (4 fl oz/120 ml)

Refined coconut oil, ½ cup
(4 fl oz/120 ml) melted

Unsweetened nondairy chocolate,
1 oz (30 g), melted

Vanilla extract, 1 tablespoon

FOR THE MOCHA LAYER

Unsweetened nondairy milk,
¼ cup (2 fl oz/60 ml)

Instant coffee grounds, 2 tablespoons

Refined coconut oil, ¼ cup
(2 fl oz/60 ml) melted

Organic powdered sugar, 1 cup
(4 oz/115 g)

FOR THE GANACHE

Coconut milk, ¼ cup (2 fl oz/60 ml)

Semisweet nondairy chocolate,
3 oz (90 g)

1. Preheat the oven to 350°F (180°C). Line a 9-inch (23-cm) square baking pan with parchment paper.

2. To make the brownies, in a large bowl, whisk together the flour, cocoa powder, sugar, arrowroot, baking powder, and ½ teaspoon salt until well combined. Whisk until well combined, making sure there are no lumps.

3. In a medium bowl, stir together the maple syrup, coconut milk, coconut oil, melted chocolate, and vanilla. (Don't use cold ingredients, or the chocolate will harden instead of mix in smoothly.) Stir the maple syrup mixture into the flour mixture just until mixed. Spoon the batter into the prepared pan and smooth the top.

4. Bake until the top looks cracked and dry, about 30 minutes. The middle should be slightly underbaked. Cool in the pan on a rack. Refrigerate the cooled brownies until completely chilled.

5. Meanwhile, to make the mocha layer, in a medium bowl, stir together the nondairy milk and coffee grounds until dissolved. Stir in the coconut oil until smooth, then stir in the powdered sugar. Once you have a spreadable paste, spread evenly over the cold brownies. Refrigerate while you make the ganache.

6. To make the ganache, in a saucepan, warm the coconut milk over low heat. Add the chopped chocolate and stir until the chocolate is melted and the ganache is smooth. Drizzle the ganache over the mocha layer of the cold brownies and refrigerate until the ganache is firm. Cut the pan of chilled brownies into 9 squares. The brownies can be stored, tightly covered in the refrigerator, for up to 1 week.

MAKES 9 BROWNIES

STRAWBERRY "CHEESE" CAKE

If you crave a creamy, over-the-top dessert, this is the one for you. Instead of using the standard cream cheese and sour cream, you'll transform silken tofu into a dense, rich treat. Coconut cream and oil give the cake a luscious creaminess.

FOR THE CRUST

Walnuts, 1 cup (4 oz/115 g)

Graham cracker crumbs, 1 cup (3 oz/90 g)

Coconut oil, ¼ cup (2 fl oz/60 ml), plus more for the pan

Maple syrup, 3 tablespoons

Sea salt

FOR THE FILLING

Firm silken tofu, 1½ lb (680 g)

Organic sugar, 1⅓ cups (12 oz/340 g)

Coconut cream, 1 cup (8 fl oz/225 ml)

Refined coconut oil, ½ cup (4 fl oz/120 ml), melted

Arrowroot, ¼ cup (1¼ oz/35 g)

Lemon zest, grated, 2 tablespoons

Lemon juice, 3 tablespoons

Nutritional yeast, 2 tablespoons

Vanilla extract, 1 tablespoon

Sea salt

FOR THE TOPPING

Strawberries, fresh or frozen, 1 lb (450 g), hulled and halved

Organic sugar, ½ cup (3½ oz/100 g)

Apple juice, ¼ cup (2 fl oz/60 ml)

Arrowroot, 1 tablespoon

Almond extract, ¼ teaspoon

1. Preheat the oven to 350°F (180°C). Coat a 9-inch (23-cm) springform pan with coconut oil.

2. To make the crust, in a food processor, process the walnuts until finely ground. Add the graham cracker crumbs, coconut oil, maple syrup, and ¼ teaspoon salt and pulse until just combined. Firmly press into the bottom of the prepared pan. Bake until set but not browned, about 10 minutes. Cool on a wire rack for 10 minutes.

3. To make the filling, drain the tofu and transfer to a blender or food processor. Blend until smooth, scraping down once or twice. Add the sugar, coconut cream, coconut oil, arrowroot, lemon zest, lemon juice, nutritional yeast, vanilla, and ¼ teaspoon salt. Blend until very smooth. Scrape into the crust.

4. Place the pan on a rimmed baking sheet and bake until the edges are golden and the center jiggles but is not liquid, 75–90 minutes. Cool on a wire rack until room temperature, about 1 hour. Refrigerate, uncovered, until very cold, at least 3 hours.

5. To make the topping, in a medium saucepan, combine the strawberries and sugar over medium heat. Bring to a boil, stirring often. Meanwhile, in a small bowl, stir together the apple juice and arrowroot. When the strawberries are softened and juicy, stir in the arrowroot mixture, then stir in the almond extract. When the mixture is thickened and glossy, pour it over the cooled cheesecake and refrigerate until cold.

6. To serve, run a sharp knife along the edge to loosen the pan sides and remove the cake. Cut into 12 wedges and serve. The cake can be stored, tightly covered in the refrigerator, for up to 4 days.

MAKES 12 SERVINGS

THE POWER OF INDIVIDUAL ACTION

Regardless of occupation, community, or age, everyone can make a difference. *It is the power of collective, individual action that brings about structural change.* In the world of food, that means using your voice and economic buying power to vote and advocate for the changes that matter to you. It also means advocating for changes that benefit others, knowing that a better food system will help every community.

Many who have seen the devastation of our current food system have already taken change into their own hands. This can be seen in the sharp growth of organic food purchases. According to the Pew Research Center, both the number of organic farms and the amount of certified organic goods sold increased by more than 50% from 2011.[1] In 2016, organic farms sold nearly $7.6 billion in certified organic goods, more than double the $3.5 billion spent in 2011.

In our own communities, there are many ways that we can spur changes in our food system. We can contact local restaurants and grocers and ask them to carry plant-based foods. We can request more labeling to help consumers make informed choices. We can help invest in and create community supported agriculture (CSA) and improve accessibility to fresh produce and affordable plant-based options.

---

[1] Bialik, Kristen, and Kristi Walker. 2019. "Organic Farming Is on the Rise in the U.S." Pew Research Center. January 10, 2019. https://www.pewresearch.org/fact-tank/2019/01/10/organic-farming-is-on-the-rise-in-the-u-s/.

But the most powerful tool in the fight for a fairer food system is our dollars. And this also means we should take the time to understand what we're buying. From the seed to the soil, to the factories, trucks and trains, shelves and labels, to our plates, every part of this journey affects us, our communities, other animals, and our world—for better or for worse.

Through your dollars, your voice, and your individual action, you can incite the change you wish to see, and collectively, we can change everything.

"Together let us join hands and hearts as we each do our bit to create a better world for our children, and theirs." [2]

---

[2] Goodall, McAvoy, and Hudson, *Harvest for Hope*, xxiv.

BASICS

"I do have reasons for hope: our clever brains, the resilience of nature, the indomitable human spirit, and above all, the commitment of young people when they're empowered to take action." —Jane

AQUAFABA AIOLI

Don't pour that chickpea water down the drain! It is the secret ingredient for a mayonnaise that rivals any jarred mayo from the grocery store. Real handmade mayonnaise is made by whipping oil into raw egg yolks. Drawing upon the amazingly eggy qualities of whipped aquafaba, you can create the same kind of emulsion and use it as a spread or dip.

Raw cashews, ¼ cup (1¼ oz/35 g)

Aquafaba, ¼ cup (2 fl oz/60 ml)

Garlic, 2 cloves, sliced

Lemon juice, 1 tablespoon

Vegan mustard, 2 teaspoons

Sea salt

Avocado oil, ½ cup (4 fl oz/120 ml)

Fresh flat-leaf parsley,
2 tablespoons minced

MAKES ABOUT
¾ CUP (180 ML)

1. Put the cashews in a heatproof bowl. Pour boiling water over the cashews and let stand until the cashews can easily be crushed with your finger, at least 2 hours. Drain well.

2. In a powerful blender, combine the cashews, aquafaba, garlic, lemon juice, mustard, and ½ teaspoon salt. Blend, starting on a lower speed and increasing to high, until the mixture is a smooth paste, scraping down as needed.

3. When the mixture is smooth, blend for 4 minutes, starting on low and increasing to high. Then remove the center cap from the lid and very slowly drizzle in the oil in a thin stream. It should take a couple of minutes to incorporate. Scrape down if you need to. When it's emulsified, add the parsley and blend to mix.

4. Scrape the aioli into a storage container or jar and refrigerate. It will thicken as it chills. The aioli can be stored, tightly covered in the refrigerator, for up to 1 week.

CAULIFLOWER-CASHEW QUESO

Many of our favorite Mexican dishes are topped with melted cheese or drizzled with sour cream. Break away from all that dairy with this savory, slightly spicy plant-based queso dip. Creamy cashews and cauliflower combine to create a smooth, pourable sauce flavored with smoke and spices, ready for nachos. Remember to soak the cashews the night before so they will purée easily.

Avocado oil or refined coconut oil, 2 tablespoons

Yellow onion, ½ cup (2 oz/60 g) chopped

Garlic, 2 cloves, chopped

Jalapeño chiles, 2, seeded and chopped

Ground cumin, 1 teaspoon

Smoked paprika, ½ teaspoon

Ground turmeric, ¼ teaspoon

Unsweetened nondairy milk, 1½ cups (12 fl oz/350 ml)

Nutritional yeast, 2 tablespoons

White miso, 2 tablespoons

Cauliflower, 2 cups (8 oz/225 g) chopped

Raw cashews, ½ cup (2 oz/60 g), soaked overnight and drained

Kimchi brine, 2 tablespoons

Apple cider vinegar, 1 teaspoon

Sea salt

MAKES 3 CUPS (700 ML)

1. In a large sauté pan, warm the oil over medium-high heat. Add the onion, garlic, and half of the chopped jalapeño and cook, stirring occasionally and reducing the heat as the onion mixture starts to sizzle, until soft and golden, about 5 minutes. Add the cumin, paprika, and turmeric and stir for a few seconds. Add the nondairy milk, nutritional yeast, miso, and cauliflower, raise the heat to high, and bring to a boil. Cover, reduce the heat to low, and cook until the cauliflower is very tender, about 10 minutes.

2. Carefully transfer the contents of the pan to a blender. Add the cashews, kimchi brine, vinegar, and 1 teaspoon salt. Cover tightly and blend until very smooth, scraping down and repeating as needed. Stir in the remaining chopped jalapeño and serve right away. The queso can be stored, tightly covered in the refrigerator, for up to 4 days.

ALMOND "CHÈVRE"

The key to making a nut-based alternative is to use fermentation in a similar way as traditional cheese. In this "chèvre," you'll grind softened soaked almonds to a smooth purée, then add the contents of a vegan probiotic capsule. Those microbes will go to work fermenting the nuts, adding a tangy taste.

Slivered almonds, 1½ cups (7 oz/200 g), soaked overnight and drained

Vegan probiotic capsule, 1, emptied out, case discarded

Nutritional yeast, 1 tablespoon (optional)

Unpasteurized apple cider vinegar, 1 teaspoon

Sea salt

MAKES 1½ CUPS (190 G)

1. In a powerful blender or food processor, mince the almonds. Add ½ cup (4 fl oz/120 ml) water and the acidophilus and blend until very smooth. Scrape down and repeat to get all the little chunks completely puréed. Transfer the mixture to a storage container or bowl and cover loosely with a towel. Let stand at room temperature for 24–48 hours. The mixture will look bubbly. (This will go more quickly in a warmer room.)

2. Taste a bit of the "chèvre" at this point. The top may look a little dry and there will be bubbles throughout. It should smell a little bready and taste a little tangy. If it isn't happening, give it another day. Stir in the nutritional yeast (if using), vinegar, and 1 teaspoon salt. The "chèvre" can be stored, tightly covered in thein the refrigerator, for up to 1 week.

SLOW-COOKER SEITAN

Making your own seitan is easy in the slow cooker, now that gluten flour, also called vital wheat gluten, is available in stores. Thanks to its spongy yet firm texture, it absorbs flavorful sauces and broths, and can be stir-fried or seared without breaking up. Try it in stews, wraps, noodle bowls, and stir-frys!

Gluten flour (vital wheat gluten), 2 cups (8½ oz/240 g)

Chickpea flour, ¼ cup (30 g)

Extra-virgin olive oil, 2 tablespoons

Tamari, 2 tablespoons

Red miso, 2 tablespoons

Tomato paste, 1 tablespoon

Dried mushrooms (any kind), 4 large (¾ oz/20 g)

Garlic, 4 cloves, halved

Tamari, 1 tablespoon

MAKES 2½ LB (1.1 KG)

1. In a large bowl, whisk together the gluten flour and chickpea flour. In a medium bowl, whisk together 1 cup (8 fl oz/250 ml) water, the oil, tamari, red miso, and tomato paste until smooth. Stir into the gluten mixture until it forms a firm dough. Knead until spongy, about 2 minutes. Form into a log about 9 inches (23 cm) long.

2. In a slow cooker, combine 8 cups (64 fl oz/1.9 l) water, the mushrooms, garlic, and tamari. Add the seitan log and, if needed, more water to cover the log. Secure the lid and cook on low for 6 hours. (Alternatively, combine the ingredients in a large pot over low heat and simmer, covered, for about 2 hours.)

3. The seitan will be firm when pressed, and should register 180°F (82°C) when an instant-read thermometer is inserted. Let cool completely in the broth, then slice, cube, or mince as needed. It can be cubed or ground and then frozen in a little broth in a tightly covered storage container. The seitan can be stored, tightly covered in the refrigerator, for up to 1 week, or in the freezer for up to 1 month.

MASA DUMPLING DOUGH

Masa harina, ½ cup (2¾ oz/80 g)

All-purpose flour, ¼ cup (1 oz/30 g)

Baking powder, ½ teaspoon

Sea salt

Cold coconut oil, 1 tablespoon, cut into small pieces

Unsweetened nondairy milk, 6 tablespoons (3 fl oz/90 ml), or more as needed

Fresh cilantro, 1 tablespoon finely chopped

MAKES ABOUT
18 DUMPLINGS

In a bowl, whisk together the masa, flour, baking powder, and ½ teaspoon salt. Using your fingertips, rub the coconut oil into the flour mixture until finely crumbled. Add the nondairy milk and cilantro and stir gently until the dough comes together. If the dough seems dry, add a little more nondairy milk, 1 teaspoon at a time.

MASA DOUGH FOR SOPES

Masa harina, 1½ cups (8¼ oz/235 g)

Chili powder, 1 teaspoon

Sea salt

Warm water (120°F/49°C), 1 cup (8 fl oz/240 ml)

MAKES DOUGH
FOR 12 SOPES

In a bowl, whisk together the masa, chile powder, and ½ teaspoon salt. Add the warm water and knead until the dough is smooth and no longer sticky. Divide the dough into 12 golf ball–size pieces. Cover with a damp towel and set aside for 10 minutes before shaping.

SPICED TOAST POINTS

Whole-wheat bread (day-old is fine), 6 slices

Extra-virgin olive oil, 2 tablespoons

Garlic, 1 clove, pressed

Ground cumin, 1 teaspoon

Paprika, ½ teaspoon

MAKES 24 TOASTS

Preheat the oven to 400°F (200°C). Have ready a rimmed baking sheet. Place the bread slices, in stacks of 2, on a cutting board and cut each stack corner to corner, and then again, to make 4 triangles from each piece of bread. In a small bowl, stir together the oil, garlic, cumin, and paprika. Use a pastry brush to lightly coat the slices on both sides with the oil mixture then place on the baking sheet. Bake for 4 minutes, then flip the toasts and and bake until the toasts are crisp, about 4 minutes more.

RÉMOULADE

Vegan mayonnaise, ¾ cup (180 ml) (or Aquafaba Aioli, page 156)

Small dill pickles, ¼ cup (1½ oz/40 g) minced, or ¼ cup (1½ oz/40 g) relish

Capers, 1 tablespoon drained

Garlic, 1 clove, pressed

Fresh flat-leaf parsley, ¼ cup (⅓ oz/10 g) finely minced

Green onion, 1, minced

Tomato paste, 1 tablespoon

Lemon juice, 1 tablespoon

Tabasco sauce, 1 teaspoon

MAKES 1 CUP
(8 FL OZ/230 ML)

Place the vegan mayonnaise in a small bowl. Add the pickles, capers, garlic, parsley, green onion, tomato paste, lemon juice, and Tabasco and stir until combined. The rémoulade can be stored, tightly covered in the refrigerator, for up to 2 days.

INDEX

#EATMEATLESS

Conceived and produced by Weldon Owen International

A WELDON OWEN PRODUCTION

PO Box 3088
San Rafael, CA 94912
www.weldonowen.com

NewSeed Press
is an imprint of Weldon Owen International

Copyright ©2021 Weldon Owen
All rights reserved, including the right of
reproduction in whole or in part in any form.

Printed in China
10 9 8 7 6 5 4 3 2 1

Library of Congress
Cataloging-in-Publication data is available.

ISBN: 978-1-68188-537-7

WELDON OWEN INTERNATIONAL

CEO Raoul Goff
Publisher Roger Shaw
Associate Publisher Amy Marr
Editorial Assistant Jourdan Plautz
Creative Director Chrissy Kwasnik
Designer Lola Villanueva

Managing Editor Lauren LePera
Production Manager Binh Au

Photographer Erin Scott
Food Stylist Lillian Kang
Prop Stylist Claire Mack

Recipes by Robin Asbell

Additional photography by:
Bill Wallauer (page 8); Thomas Mangelsen
(pages 13, 19, 37, 94, 136); Shutterstock (pages
16, 38); Roy Borghouts (page 22); Getty Images
(page 60); Jane Goodall Institute/Roots & Shoots
(page 154); and Michael Collopy (back cover)

Weldon Owen wishes to thank the following for
their generous support in producing this book:
Dr. Jane Goodall, Jane Goodall Institute USA, Kris Balloun,
Lesley Bruynesteyn, Rachel Markowitz, and Elizabeth Parson.